# Transparent Moments

## S.B. Jinkins

Transparent Moments
© S.B.Jinkins 2024

All rights reserved. No part of this publication may be reproduced, stored in a retrieval system, or transmitted in any form or by any means, electronic, mechanical, photocopying, recording or otherwise, without the prior written permission of the author.

ISBN:    978-1-923163-66-9

 A catalogue record for this work is available from the National Library of Australia

Cover Design: Clark & Mackay
Format and Typeset: Clark & Mackay
Self-Published by S.B.Jinkins with assistance from Clark & Mackay

Proudly printed in Australia by Clark & Mackay

*With much love to the three Dawn's in my life and my wonderful sister-in-law Roniece.*

# Contents

A Question to Ms Minerva Chapman . . . . . . . . . . . . . . . . . . . . . . . . . . . 1
A Smile . . . . . . . . . . . . . . . . . . . . . . . . . . . . . . . . . . . . . . . . . . . . . . . . 3
A Discourse on Happiness . . . . . . . . . . . . . . . . . . . . . . . . . . . . . . . . . . 4
45th Street . . . . . . . . . . . . . . . . . . . . . . . . . . . . . . . . . . . . . . . . . . . . . . 6
All That Jazz . . . . . . . . . . . . . . . . . . . . . . . . . . . . . . . . . . . . . . . . . . . . 7
Alzheimer's . . . . . . . . . . . . . . . . . . . . . . . . . . . . . . . . . . . . . . . . . . . . . 8
At some particular point in her life, she paused . . . . . . . . . . . . . . . . . 9
Archives and Memories . . . . . . . . . . . . . . . . . . . . . . . . . . . . . . . . . . 10
A Wee Tale About a Lord and a King . . . . . . . . . . . . . . . . . . . . . . . 12
Azure Sky . . . . . . . . . . . . . . . . . . . . . . . . . . . . . . . . . . . . . . . . . . . . . 16
Because I Can . . . . . . . . . . . . . . . . . . . . . . . . . . . . . . . . . . . . . . . . . 18
Black Hollyhock . . . . . . . . . . . . . . . . . . . . . . . . . . . . . . . . . . . . . . . 20
Brother Lost . . . . . . . . . . . . . . . . . . . . . . . . . . . . . . . . . . . . . . . . . . 22
Burnt at the stake for a crime I didn't commit . . . . . . . . . . . . . . . . 23
A celebrity's fathomless eyes . . . . . . . . . . . . . . . . . . . . . . . . . . . . . . 25
Checkers Witch . . . . . . . . . . . . . . . . . . . . . . . . . . . . . . . . . . . . . . . . 26
Constant . . . . . . . . . . . . . . . . . . . . . . . . . . . . . . . . . . . . . . . . . . . . . 28
Something Almost Like Unrequited Lust . . . . . . . . . . . . . . . . . . . . 29
Reformed Smoker's Pledge . . . . . . . . . . . . . . . . . . . . . . . . . . . . . . . 31
Damned Stupid Man . . . . . . . . . . . . . . . . . . . . . . . . . . . . . . . . . . . 32
Dance . . . . . . . . . . . . . . . . . . . . . . . . . . . . . . . . . . . . . . . . . . . . . . . 33
When Humanity Speaks to a Sad Child Following a Lonely Path . . . . . . . . 34
Deadheading the Roses . . . . . . . . . . . . . . . . . . . . . . . . . . . . . . . . . . 35
Dionysus and the Island . . . . . . . . . . . . . . . . . . . . . . . . . . . . . . . . . 36
Door-To-Door Salesman . . . . . . . . . . . . . . . . . . . . . . . . . . . . . . . . 37
Drought of 05 . . . . . . . . . . . . . . . . . . . . . . . . . . . . . . . . . . . . . . . . . 38
Eyes that echo on a windowpane . . . . . . . . . . . . . . . . . . . . . . . . . . 40

Ferdinand the Bull ... 42
Fistfuls of Mud ... 46
For Bella ... 47
Gardener's Delight ... 48
For Papa—A Lament ... 49
Give It Your Best Shot ... 50
Glory Days ... 52
Groundhog Day ... 54
Rainbow With Black as a Shadow ... 56
Heartland ... 57
Home at War ... 58
Hope is that intangible thing ... 59
I am glass ... 60
In Defence of the Middle-Aged Woman in Baudelaire's "Windows" Portrait ... 61
Fear Not ... 63
Dad ... 64
I am Woman (To Mum) ... 66
If I ... 67
The Death of a Fawn and the Canvas Created ... 68
Impressions of Insanity—up close and personal ... 69
Joy—A Lament ... 70
Joy ... 72
Judgement ... 73
Kafka, Me, and Bobby McGee ... 74
Kate ... 76
My friend Kate ... 77
Kookaburra Calling ... 88
Lake Song ... 89
Sweet Dreams ... 90

| | |
|---|---|
| Letter to My Son | 91 |
| Logs Stacked | 93 |
| Losing Time | 94 |
| Lullaby | 95 |
| Marathon Man | 96 |
| Masquerade | 98 |
| Mates | 99 |
| Mea Culpa | 100 |
| Mockery Unplugged | 101 |
| Mother and Child | 102 |
| No-World | 103 |
| O Jealousy | 106 |
| Ode to the Hugo Boss Man | 108 |
| Old Man | 109 |
| One Tear | 110 |
| Open Arms | 112 |
| Plastic Fantastic | 113 |
| Pretensions of Poetry | 114 |
| Protest song against dictatorship | 115 |
| Rain Chant | 117 |
| Reclusive Silence | 118 |
| Refinement | 120 |
| Rosebud | 121 |
| Self-Doubt and Communication | 122 |
| Shh—The world need not know | 124 |
| Simple Love Poem | 126 |
| States of Matter | 127 |
| Table Talk | 128 |
| Terminals—Flights | 129 |
| Dedication to the Aspen Tree | 130 |

| | |
|---|---|
| The Clown | 131 |
| The Disappeared | 132 |
| The Family | 134 |
| The Forgotten | 135 |
| Impressionists | 137 |
| The Joker | 138 |
| The Liverpool Kid | 139 |
| Ode to the Working Mum | 140 |
| The man who carried round his neatly wrapped box | 142 |
| The Pond | 143 |
| The Tree | 144 |
| The Moth, the Moon, and the False Light | 146 |
| Immersion | 147 |
| There Was a Boy | 148 |
| Retro | 149 |
| Thursday: 8.00 pm | 150 |
| Transparent Moments | 152 |
| Unrequited Lust | 153 |
| Vincent | 154 |
| Birds of a Feather | 155 |
| When a Man Despises a Woman and Vice Versa | 160 |
| When one has lived a long time within the maddening crowd | 162 |
| Woman to Woman | 164 |
| Worm performing the capoeira while I'm hanging out the washing | 165 |
| Yesterday's News | 167 |
| If Only | 168 |
| Chess Pieces | 169 |

# A Question to Ms Minerva Chapman

*Dear Minerva, please tell me what is the simplest possible condition?*

Is it the small ebony seed nestled in a cocoon of white,
wispy, candy-floss bolls,
Thirsty for water and sunlight then made ripe for the picking?

Or the dark days of the "Cotton Kings",
the backbone of Southern American pride,
People with freedom denied; bound, traded, enslaved, and
dispatched to the history books under H for "holocaust"?

Or the blank canvas; stretched taut, prepped ...
waiting for that exquisite sound,
The first sweep of the sable brush—a sigh made by the artist's hand.

Or the artist who waits doggedly for the canvas to speak first—
The paint pots lined up in haphazard fashion humming an alluring tune,
Jiggling incessantly to be converted onto the pure canvas?

Or the piece of art capturing centre stage/
a vision of colour/pure lines/simplistic/
almost childlike in form/showing a mastery of technique
critics-admirers gush/
an artist starving for acceptance/or a child playing with crayons?

Or that stray thought, feeling, look, carefully hidden—
not available for display.
A stubborn inconvenient infestation that casts a
small shadow on the heart?

*I wonder, Ms Minerva—if it's any of the above?*

# A Smile

A smile is a silent laugh.
The lips curve upwards to convey ...
The joy of a moment captured in time.
A light-hearted gesture between friends,
A sympathetic signal of some understanding,
A child's fun-filled innocent delight,
The feel of a warm breeze touching the face,
The majestic sight of Nature at peace,
A cheerful greeting to brighten up one's day.
A smile is all these things, it's true—
But most of all, it's that magical connection between me and you,
That magical connection that binds us all.

# A Discourse on Happiness

There was a baby boy.
There was a baby girl.
Released from the sanctity of their mother's womb,
One after another.

People would see them in their pram,
To cluck and coo and stretch over to view
The baby boy with twin pools of sorrowful eyes,
The baby girl with shining wells of wonder.

When they went to school,
An experiment was contrived
In the interests of state and matter
To assess the contents of a glass container.

"Don't you see, the glass is half-empty,"
Stated the boy, rather emphatically.
The girl felt very confused;
All she could see was the glass half-full.

Through their teenage years, with growing pains
The boy went in search of an indefinable state of being.
He yearned to smile, feel happiness well up inside,
To have it reflected in his eyes.

The girl's joy and wonder that had dwelled within,
Naturally displayed by her champagne eyes,
Encountered the rough realities of life.
Her eyes became flat; that essence of light simply died a little inside.

So they both lived into middle age.
The brother and sister became reacquainted again.
Curiously, there was a discernible shaft of light
Now visible in both pairs of eyes.

They smiled at each other, filled with genuine delight
As they realised uncontrived emotion cannot be ignored
Given the right climate of mind—it can burst its way through
As treasured, transient moments of happiness.

# 45th Street

1
The streets of New York,
Vibrant, crowded, staunch, defiant.
Snowflakes falling,
A midwinter's day.
A beggar sitting on a concrete step
Outside a place of worship.
Lightly clad,
With a sign by her side:
"Please help feed my children …
We have no place to live."
I sit down to converse,
Wrapped in my own security blanket.
Offer a sympathetic ear,
Not prepared for the harsh reality
Of a city that offers no help
For its people that fall by the wayside.

2
She is clear-eyed.
A lone figure sitting on her pride.
Knocked away the offer of a cigarette,
An abused wife
Who hadn't picked up enough welfare points?
On the run from her demented spouse
A person who has been through a traumatic experience,
Much like the city itself.
*Her own private 9/11*
*With no resolution in sight.*

# All That Jazz

You closed a can of worms
When you said goodbye.
The saxophonist did his opening solo,
Couldn't shake the blues,
With all that jazz.
Your mind lingered longer
While your body took a left.
I quelled any dread
As your shadow disappeared.
I wished your face would melt away, too,
As I stare into the memory of your eyes.
Cats eye, with nine lives,
Remembering the feel of your ebony skin.
My body of works
Touched by your half-baked lies.
Your hands made intricate designs,
Wild man, savage heart,
Worn inside out.
Interesting on all levels.
Left to wonder maybe
If there was a possibility
You'd ever tame that heart.

## Alzheimer's

When I asked you to return
In recollection of remembrance,
You searched for your mate instead,
But insight was not to be found.
As with Ted Hughes' crows,
In deepest grief, you flew and flew
Into the bleak, black nights of the mind.
I cradle your still form in wonderment,
Searching for some clue as to
The twin deaths of thought and memory.

Time moves on.
You are long since dead.
The crevices and cracks of my mind
Seem to form a shadow.
It's the elephant in the room …
Now I do not know who I am,
Nor what you might have been to me.

# At some particular point in her life, she paused

At some particular point in her life, she paused
And was gripped by a sorrow.
She wondered if what was once would ever be again.
The blackened shell of night offered up no respite;
The moon had long since ceased to be her friend.
The passing parade of faces
Lurched unmasked to reveal no mystery,
Just a shallow sea of ships plain sailing.

In Her mind He had taken up squatter rights
And offered up no apology.
He had moved on
To another sacrificial flame
That would burn bright,
Lit up by fingertips and soft lies
Until desire was doused by escape plans.

He'd stopped long enough
To leave the remnants of a T-shirt behind.
Ripped apart by her raw hands,
Tobacco smoke and whispered words
Mingled in amongst the cotton shreds.
The threads lightly teased her frostbitten face.
She laid them gently on the grate
And watched them dance on fire.
Her eyes sunk back into pools of ice,
It would be a hell of a long time
Before she'd pause again.

## Archives and Memories

Its words, music, pictures,
That dance before my eyes
Oh, learned professor.
As you take the time
To seek, uncover, explore, decipher,
You're hunting treasures.
Carefully wrapping them in brown paper,
Placing them in the blue-green opaque bottle,
Launching them into the restless water.

I, like the others, await the drift to shore.
The content is released.
It allows us to contemplate, consider,
Absorb the archives, ruminate on the intent.
Be baffled or filled with wonder.
It is art; selected with care,
Passed on with selfless regard,
That always manages to be squirreled away
In a small place within our hearts.

But it is your memories
That are my greatest delight.
Your treasures that speak of chance encounters,
Places seen and heard.
The thoughts, fears, and joys,
A peek, if you will ...
At the complexity of your mind.
What draws your breath, what pulls you up short
To simply gaze with awe.

Intellect or Art,
Who would have thought?
Two states able to coincide, to provide
The delicious impressions that you are.
So I take these memories and store them away.
They don't occupy a place in my heart.
They reach down and merge rhythmically
As part of my soul.

# A Wee Tale About a Lord and a King

**1**

'Twas on the night of 1310; two foes stood toe to toe in the great hall of Gloucester, where debauching and feasting were partaken aplenty.

One, an English liege of great intellect, dressed all in a brocade of finery. The other, draped in a *lèine* of coarse darkest brown, a self-appointed Scottish king.

*"'Tis a war I bryng to yer dore! Ye'll no see daylicht 'til ma tongue isna unner yer belt. Freeman stand—tyrant fall!"*

The green eyes of the people's king reflected the wrath of a thousand blasphemes. The liege stood silent with anger raised but inbred regal regard. The gathered noblemen were all a-twitter; how dare this wild man, dressed as womenfolk, speak with words that were ill understood!

'Twas a vow the "Liege of Letters" took then to learn the tongue of the Scottish blackguard. He longed for the bounty of parchments by the hearth and, all at once a dither with a mix of pain and anger, he made haste the foe's safe passage to a wee border town.

But 'twas with a heavy heart that the order from Edward "Longshanks" came to mind.

*"All speed must be given and no quarter spared to quell the feral beast known as Scotland"*

# 2

Many a morn and night did follow, whereupon the English army made true the orders of their king. The English foe ravaged and razed the land; bloodlust flowed through every village, Fife, loch, and glen. The wee *barnes'* eyes carried the rabid fear of the "Scarlet Rose"; the womenfolk shouldered the labours of men and suffered a horrid ravishing. The clan's men, with verily little but pride and the rugged illusory terrain, fought and fell with a fever of disdain.

Hunted and harried, the people's king so dragged his dimming force and battle-weary body to a craggy retreat. Thereupon being the hand of fate, sad tidings were received that his dearest of kin had suffered a grievous demise by none other than the most learned of men—the noble liege. 'Twas the soulful song of the pan flute and the howl of deepest despair that rent the air that night—what misery 'tis the pay o' freedom!

Thereupon he lay naked on a wooden cot, bare to the chill wind, a sacrifice to the raging fires of despair. Through the mist of malaise, a spider he did spy; strand after silken strand that would nay stick. The creature fell but six times and an oath he did swear: "'Tis be six times we Scots did fall; if the spider do succeed on the seventh, 'tis a sign to bring forth the forces of Minerva to resist the English spite once and for all." And before his eyes, the creature made true the fate. 'Twas with a stiffened spine that the pauper king did rise; 'tis with glory and gore he'd meet his demise!

## 3

On a hot, wet morn in the month of June, the warrior king took his stand on the road from Falkirk, northward over the *burn* to the castle gates of Sterling. So they gathered: Lothian men and borderers, Gall-Gaels from Galloway, Scoto-Picts from Fife, and spearman from Moray and Ross. Sat tall on a Punch pony, he set his schiltrons with cunning and skill, protecting his front with pits and traps, ten score deadly caltrops to the flanks, and the low, swampy cover of New Park. The time was nigh; with fewer than a quart of Longshank's men, he set his four divisions as a mighty shield—and lay in wait over the Bannock Burn.

'Twas a colourful array that greeted the clansmen that day. The burnished glint of English armour with the knights sat proud and straight on splendid English steeds. Nary a muscle did move; the line stayed true as the sound of thunderous hooves charged toward them. The crack could be heard all over the land as the horses did fall and the English army did impale upon the pikemen. The battle did rage all the day, the ground soaked blood-red with the entrails of both beast and human. The warrior king set a final ruse that tricked the mortal foe, so believing they were all but defeated, but all at once—with a cunning retort—rose up with the might of Colossus!

In the throes of victory, the warrior king happened upon the liege with a nasty gash, desperate to fight off the intent of three clansmen. 'Twas a skill the liege did show with sword in hand, cursing them loud in the Scottish tongue. A moment the king did take before he shouted, "Halt!" whereupon the three clansmen did cease and desist.

Stunned, they looked at him, upon which the king did retort *"E'enin orts is guid mornin's fother."* 'Tis with a gladness in his heart he knew the Liege did understand! As the lord limped to his escape, the words the king spoke in the English tongue did follow him ...

*"Och, mon, 'tis nowt personal—'tis 'bout givin' respect and takin' freedom."*

# Azure Sky

You ask me to lie back and describe the sky to you
Like when I was a child sprawled out in long rye grass,
So quiet, flat on my back, collecting cloud mosaics,
My eyes following their patterned progress,
Feeling so small but wanting the sky to offer up more.

Is it a presumption on my part?
A sense you want me to view the sky like you?
All azure with dreams of quiet contemplation,
A warm, cosy protective blanket,
Monochrome with no coloured relief
Covering the earth with flat-feathered grace.

I want to see the sun,
That glorious light offered up
In bursts of linear streams
Splintered by the long rye stems
With their ragged seed heads.

I want the rock and roll of a storm,
To hear that cantankerous drumbeat,
Watch the tentacles that reach out
Sizzling and sluicing with a
Surgical knife-edge display.

I want to see the moon
Punching holes through the sky,
Reaching down to me
With no compromise
To caress and envelop me.

Is it too much to ask
To view the sky as a portal to the stars?
Imaginary worlds that may seem real,
Where the impossible becomes challengeable?
Minds that wander through distance and time,
A multiplicity of energised diverseness.

You want me to regress, you say,
So you can better understand me.
I never did view the sky like you.
Is it so wrong to want the storm, the sun, the stars, the moon,
Instead of your pretty azure sky?

# Because I Can

It was as though things had come easily to him all his life.
Indeed, he had been anointed by success as long as he could remember.

So he stood tall on his island and surveyed the horizon,
Watching the microscopic images of humanity buzzing by.

He wanted to shout out to them, "See, I'm not lonely—just alone!"
But he knew the wind would return his words straight back again.

Yet if he stood stonily still, he fancied he could feel the world spin seductively around him, content the people still loved him because separation had been preserved.

Every day, he'd send out his sweet siren song that spoke of passion, longing, and despair.
Beautiful words placed in a bottle, floating rhythmically with the ebb and flow of the tide.

His eager believers would pick up his words and digest them, then dissect them, for that skerrick of meaning that would add a glow to their seemingly normal lives.

The most ardent among them would attempt the treacherous crossing, only to have their hearts dashed on the jagged rocks or be pushed back by the merciless tides.

He would then turn away—back to his lighthouse tower with books stacked ten high,
In search of the highest quest to determine the meaning of life.

His visitors were few, although it was said Dionysus would pop in for a chat,
But that was considered okay, because he was half god, after all.

Every now and then, he'd leave the island to ply his trade
By living in the past, present, future, playing at other people's lives.

So it was … a woman walking, with the heat hot on her back,
Spied the island among the diamonds in the water and dived in unafraid.

She swam smoothly and was confident of success—years of cynicism had cast her heart in stone, and she'd learnt long ago to swim against the tide.

She reached the island and hauled herself from the water.
He loomed over her angrily over her as if to say, "See, I'm just a man!"

As she turned back to the sea, his voice enquired softly,
"Why did you come here at all?"
She stopped, gave a whimsical smile,
and the wind carried her words back to him …

"It's simple, really—because I can."

# Black Hollyhock

A bird must have dropped you as a tiny seed in exile from the space you were meant to have in this world. Taking up your vagrant position, you nestled into the earth, oblivious to the foreignness you represented. With a calm acceptance of alien soil, you waited for the moist embryonic thrust leading to germination. Overshadowed by the surrounding plants, you were denied growth, so you paused for a time, soaked in the moisture, and imagined light. The warmth of dreams fed your ambition to pierce the skin of the soil. Gravity did the rest as you were dragged into emergence as a vulnerable radicle.

Even then, did they know you were different? You chose to ignore their whispers in veiled silence as they sought to pass judgement on you and instead focused on the push for growth, driving upwards, fighting strangeness, wanting to touch the light you had so long searched for.

The upright blooms of sanctified conservatism conversed amongst themselves and made a determination. The purity of the intellectualism that had long been cultivated was gravely at risk with such an oddity in their garden. In a show of solidarity, they moved their heads away and formed a display, hoping to expose you. But still you grew, because that's all you knew how to do, and you dreamed of a day when you would reach the full bloom of your potential.

The bed of plants chattered on endlessly about a huge, strange creature they called the Gardener. You had never seen this thing, this who they bowed to in silent communion, the beginning, the middle, and the end of their existence. You chose instead to sway with the winds as they rendered your stem vulnerable; you relished the days when the sun graced your leaves with playful tickles of light and drank deeply of the rains that re-energised your will to survive. Now filled with new sources of wonder, you failed to notice that those around you had long since ignored you in the hope you would fade away.

But instead, buds appeared, tightly clustered as though waiting for some secret signal to unfurl, answering the call of impending ripeness. One morning, when the last of the dew was sucked up by the first waves of early morning sun, one bloom tentatively sneaked a peek then, gathering strength, stretched out as wide and as proud as possible. The bedding plants turned their heads skywards and gaped in stunned silence. Then a chorus of gasps issued forth as their moment of dread had finally been realised.

"That you should grow so quiet, so strong, so black and so tall, when clearly you don't belong here, is unacceptable," said the red impatiens who took a leadership role.

Then, in that moment, all the joy you felt in being you finally came to a head and you spoke in a clear, composed voice. "You denied me light when I needed it most, you called me different without knowing why, you turned away in the hope I would fade away, and as I stand before you, you openly gasp with dread. Yes, I am as different to you as night from day, but all I have ever shown you is respect. So, please behold; I will take my moment in the sun, I will relish all my blooms that unfurl and, when that moment comes, I will let my seed spread all over the ground. So, someday, perhaps your Gardner will see the power of One because, before the summer comes to an end, you will shrivel up in your annual decay, but please know I will live on perennially."

## Brother Lost

I last saw you twenty-three years ago,
I just want to know
Are you walking on this earth somewhere?
Your family can't find you,
So where are you, my brother?
Why don't we know?
Why can't we reach you?
Have you deliberately disappeared?
I don't want to think
You no longer exist.
I just want to tell you
Our father has died.
For you, perhaps, a blessing in disguise?
I hate to think you are all alone,
So why can't we reach you?
I don't want to think the unthinkable.
Mum wants to know why she's lost a son.
Please help us to find you.

# Burnt at the stake for a crime I didn't commit

My hands reach out from the incendiary flames.
I want to touch my accuser one last time.
Peer out from the oil-soaked sticks that stand sentry,
And admonish your need for any burden of proof.

*Burn her (chant); Condemn her (chant),*
*Damn her (chant); Cleanse her (chant),*
*Absolve her (chant); Possess her (chant).*

Burn me: watch my skin bubble, shrivel, fry.
Condemn me: yet I've told no lie.
Damn me: for this imaginary heretic crime.
Cleanse me: purify the actions created in your mind's eye.
Absolve me: accuser falsehood, for I know the truth.
Possess me: yet know I'll never bend to your will.

*Burn her (chant); Condemn her (chant),*
*Damn her (chant); Cleanse her (chant),*
*Absolve her (chant); Possess her (chant).*

Smell my oils feed the flames of your rebuke,
See my bones glow incandescent with rage,
Strike at the very heart of my desires,
Hear the wails of my witching songs.

*Burn her (chant); Condemn her (chant),*
*Damn her (chant); Cleanse her (chant),*
*Absolve her (chant); Possess her (chant).*

I will gaze out, still, to the red moon.
I neither desire war nor strife.
I merely die in hope some day
You'll march in my defence.

# A celebrity's fathomless eyes

If I should see you when I happen to walk down the street
and lock on to your eyes,
When they are still enough, not fighting the fear of being recognised.
I will not stare because you're important and all that, just be taken
back by the empty void that resides there.
I would be pulled in waiting for the fathomless to disappear.
But it would be a long moment before that would happen,
Before I'd land in your mind's eye, where hope did die.
Strapped to a cross of your own devotion, the masked disciple of narcissism
That you couldn't even remove to worship at his altar,
Lest he'd see who you really are.
Fools don't rush in, they merely die—ordinary people, they and I.
So, I have a solution, nameless person.
Wear sunglasses as a tool to block ordinary people seeing
There really is no essence of you.

# Checkers Witch

"Come hither—release me"; the chant a haunting whisper
Rode on the back of the wind, with a reckless and mysterious
seduction
Into the arms of the Cross Keys Inn.

It was a merry gathering of rustic kin that greeted us then.
The fireside glowed with the promise of warmth and welcome,
Then a challenge was laid down as a decree:
A game of checkers and the right to be
Crowned Checkers Witch for the night.

Many a game was had, with wine, song, and such tales of splendour
It ignited a fire within my staid and stale mind.
On this blue moon night, I did rise an apprentice witch,
And in the morn would be anointed at Castle Rigg.

The sea of grass did sway and bend in the wind,
The waves of rye bowed in perfect unison,
But the wail of the chant could be heard louder now.
There Castle Rigg stood, magnificent, tall, and proud,
With her circle of stone daughters too numerous to count.

Her siren song lured me to the rocks,
The play of light glowed on her craggy face.
Her hoary cackle called, "Release us from this entombment that traps us for eternity."
I measure the strength of the spell and, empowered by my witchery,
Walked round the stone daughters at a measured pace.

Round and round I went, faster, faster ...
Caught up in the Castle's vortex of grief,
I spun until the blur of rocks became one.
Then, possessed by the demons of mistrust that plagued me,
Alas, I felt my inner witch spirit drain from me.

Old Jock, seemingly immune from the flow of energy,
Said in his gruff Northern tone, "If you don't trust,
She'll force you to leave summat behind."
I turned, walked barefoot along the fells.
The sun's warmth engulfed me, welcoming me home.

I smiled a secretive Checkers Witch smile.
*At least she couldn't take my heart ...*
*It had already turned to stone.*

# Constant

And I remember that time
When we sat in silent communion
Until you declared
I will be a constant in your life.
I smiled.
Constant like the light freshness of boronia
caught on a spring breeze?
"Yes," you said.
Constant like the feel of summertime
hay laying limp in the bright sunlight ready to bale?
"Of course," you said.
Constant like the blast of red that assails the eyes from crispy
autumn maple leaves?
"Sure thing," you said.
Constant like the taste of icy wintery sleet flakes caught
on the tip of the tongue?
"Most definitely," you said.
Constant in those solitary times when
I seek the arms of a lover to hold me?
How constant is constant? I inquired.
"As constant as a moment will allow," you said.
I just smiled.

# Something Almost Like Unrequited Lust

Somewhere from Sydney to LA—you must have thought of me—you called me—what was it? Did you catch a glimpse of a woman with a fringe, olive skin and a crooked smile—an image you should have left behind—you told me you missed me—I sacrificed the truth so you could no longer touch me—I said I was busy—kept the tremble from my voice—politely enquired about your wife and family?

Somewhere from LA to Boston—you must have wondered about me—you left a voice mail for me—was there something you remembered? Something so obscure—perhaps a pair of black high heels—a long red coat or maybe an encounter with a female with attitude—you said you needed me—biting the side of my lip—I only played your message once—quivered at the deep resonance of your voice—pictured your wife and family.

Somewhere from Boston to New York—I guess you had a memory of me—you emailed me—why was that? Did you go past the Italian restaurant in the heart of Manhattan, the one where you first took my hand, fed me your strange but wonderful conversation, danced along with my respect—you wrote you still wanted me—I studied your words—trembled a little—deleted them from my mind's eye—brought up an image of your picture-perfect family.

Somewhere from New York to Paris—you called me again—you spoke so softly—I hardly heard you—I caught the hesitation in your voice—then a second of silence—you told me you needed to see me—I forcefully put down the phone—took myself out into the driving rain—washed away the residue of you—bathed in my hesitation, too—thought about your wife and family. I will never be that other woman—I turned to walk home—I tested my resolve and it held—I crave the sunlight on my skin—the warm embrace of my family—I will forget you—you will forget me, too.

# Reformed Smoker's Pledge

I'm on the run …
The Big Seven have sent you
To hunt me down.
I'm but one breath away
From giving in …
My daily battle
Confronting a societal sin.
I feel you all around,
In my hair, on my clothes,
Absorbed through my skin.

Yet I left you fifteen years ago
In a fit of defiant rage.
The control you had over me
At such a young age.
Sweet remembrance of
Drawing you deeply in
Innate, yet glowing bright,
Your carcinogenic toxins
Offering a brief respite
From the hustle and bustle
Of modern life.

I still remember your seductive siren song
Curling round my lungs,
The synaptic pleasure of this legal crime.
Some say—it's only a matter of time …
But I will resist
Till my last dying breath.

# Damned Stupid Man

If you were drowning in the wake of your ignorance and deceit,
I wouldn't save you.
I'd let you sink below the surface,
Watch the bubbles of lies rise unnaturally to the top,
And then I'd calmly count them.
Unlike the way we count the thousands of innocent causalities
Who wash up on the lists of collateral damage that believe your duplicity.

Let the history books show ...
The tyrant of Stupidity, who was elevated by his party
To become the most dangerous fool of all.

# Dance

Dance for me? you ask
I throw back my head and laugh.
Mystical Pied Piper, call out your tunes,
The body's involuntary pleasure,
The desire that moves me.
Surges as a sensual beat,
So mysterious, rhythmic, pulsating,
As my hips move, echoing, in perfect unison,
And I pound the ground
In resistance to your tango, bolero bandido.
Sighs, gasps, and whispered enchantments,
Fingertip flames extend out over the distance
To run up and down, to caress and connect
Two bodies that seek a lover's sustenance.
Is this how two wonderlands collide, separate but in time?
Each takes turns to penetrate the other, absorb the heat,
Bathe in the moisture of early morning dew.
As the dance picks up in tempo,
The worlds merge, the beat intensifies, the movements explode.
Nirvana is reached; the dance is complete.

# When Humanity Speaks to a Sad Child Following a Lonely Path

Dear child, do not walk away from me.
My name is Humanity.
"But see, I have to walk away from you;
My pa beats on my ma almost every night,
My sister says I'm a scaredy cat and hates me;
The kids at school tease and shove me."

But, child, give me a chance to show you love ...
"I'd rather follow this path and see where it leads me."
But what about when darkness falls
And you find yourself all alone?
What will you do then?
"I will just cry for you."

# Deadheading the Roses

You wanted me to tell you what?
That I liked deadheading the roses
To watch them be plucked slowly then fall;
To gather them up in the palm of my hand
Wearing a gardening glove pierced from over-use
Because I didn't want to feel their decay.
Yet how is it they bloomed and I didn't notice?
Was it you who turned away from them first,
Or was it me that hung on to their bloom of promise?
Expectations came and went,
And I sigh now as the job is done.
I wash my hands, wiping away any specks of dirt
That place a stain upon my skin.
Yet still there are grains that remain unmoved,
Stuck, embedded under my nails.
It's a damnably slow process.
It is, it was, as it will always be,
Nature's curtain call,
From perfection to disintegration.
The perfume lingers in soft ripples,
Even as the scarred petals fall.
The head of the bloom is exposed,
Naked and vulnerable,
And I wait
Until the roses need deadheading again.

# Dionysus and the Island

If you were an island, I wonder?
Would you bask in the foreignness of your soil?
Tend your vines as they spill forth
The fermented grape juice
That offers up whimsy and rhapsody
To those mortal women
Who dance, enslaved in worship,
As they feed their rapture
At feverish gatherings,
Drunk on the beauty
Of well-placed verse,
Pushing on past limitations
Of your well-defined boundaries
Across the seas,
Blinded by their reflections
Coming off the water.
In their eyes, you are a demi-god.
I see you more as an island.
As their Dionysus, do you feel the separation?
Presiding over the cult of communion
Between the living and the dead.

As an island,
Is it you must stand isolated
From their feeding frenzy?
Cut out of the rock
You were created from.
I wonder does a rock ever bleed?
As an island,
Do you ever cry?

## Door-To-Door Salesman

At the age of twenty, Pete became a door-to-door salesman,
Discovered the art of fast-talking and gentle persuasion.
Honed his selling skills and made the Guinness Book of Records
For most closures in a year,
Becoming a legend amongst the League of Gentlemen.

By age thirty, he had moved into corporate selling,
Refined his sales pitch, and discovered the art of networking.
The restaurant became his office,
The hotel his residence;
He was well onto wife number two.

By age forty, he had remarried again,
Having acquired the art of fast-living.
Traded on his reputation,
Learnt to lie straight in bed,
Forgot the art of selling.

By age fifty, with three ex-wives,
Sucked dry by payments of alimony,
Had a heart attack, laid him flat on his back,
Became a born-again Christian.
Discovered he'd sold his soul to survive.

# Drought of 05

Cry for me, great lady,
Shed your tears upon the land.
An ochre hue engulfs the earth.
Only jaded thistles remain.

Every day, eyes turn skyward.
Our compulsive ritual
A pilgrimage of despair:
Staggery cows,
Eczema-ridden sheep,
Maggots devour the carcass of a stillborn lamb.

Oh, fickle lady,
You deal a ruthless hand.
Storm clouds with flashes of brilliance,
Yet only a few drops fall.

Anticipation rising,
Replaced with despair.
Oh, Mother of this earth,
Don't desert us in our hour of need.
We are but children of a lesser God.
Please hear my silent prayer.

I yearn for the vibrance of green,
The smell of freshly mowed hay.
Nature's store in abundance,
The soft sweep of rain on my face.

Yet still we persevere,
People of the land,
Our homes and livelihoods entwined.
Neither in control,
Temporary trustees
For what you have planned.

# Eyes that echo on a windowpane

Your eyes tell a story.
Let me turn the creases of the pages
With the echoes of soft rain on a windowpane
In the blink of your fathomless eyes.

You are the strong adventurer gazing out with boldness,
Looking back with vague interest,
Stalking the pages of the feminine mystique
To haunt the recesses of their fertile imaginations.

But don't I see a glimpse of timidity
That surfaces from the inner-child.
An eternal lost soul caught in the unrelenting
Hustle and bustle of the shrill neon lights.

Occasionally, the playful child's pause of innocence
Bubbles to the surface, to peer out unafraid
With hues of Turkish sweetness
Ushering in joyful, childish baubles of delight.

But I also sense the grey dusk of sorrow
Of an incomplete story, so fragile,
Searching for the unquenchable, unreachable, the intangible,
An elusive quest for meaning and substance within life.

Sometimes, you shoulder the weariness of the early pioneer
That looks out with longing on the open untamed frontier
And dream dreams of stealing progress against a harsh reality
With only the nurtured spirit of maternal memories to comfort you.

But the artist's perspective offers up a faceted vision:
The brooding menace of Brando,
The complexity of Modigliani,
The whimsy of Norma Jean,
The compassion of Proust.

Your eyes may tell a story,
But it's your indomitable spirit that remains real.
With the echoes of soft rain on a windowpane,
Can we ever really know?

# Ferdinand the Bull

I went walking to the Papuas to get my horse, Kate. Barry seemed intent on me walking around the long way, and soon it became apparent why. There, lying on the bike track, was the small outline of what could only be described as a distortion of a calf. Still. A pathetic creature. A tiny smooth caucus with only the semblance of fur, lying in the insipid winter sunlight. It turned out to be a he, with only the slightest featherlike movement from the rib cage to indicate life. I looked at Barry that way I always did when nature presented a challenge, and he went, "Oh shit, Susan; you don't expect me to carry this all the way to the calf shed, do you?"

"Yep," I said. "I sure do."

"But this has to be the ugliest thing I've ever seen."

"Yeah, I know, but how long has he been out here lying like this in the middle of winter, and he's still alive?" I demanded.

"A day or so," he mumbled.

"Then he has a will and deserves the chance to live." I was resolute, and that was the end of that.

Barry carried that dead weight for a kilometre or so, and for him, it must have seemed an eternity. I decided in my own mind to call him "Calf", because his odds of survival were next to none, but I was damned annoyed that poor Calf had been abandoned by everyone.

The calf shed was a concrete monstrosity that didn't lend itself to the harsh winter winds that whistled through it, so I set Calf down in a cocoon of hay and started a program of feeding him every four hours. I thought if I could replicate, after a fashion, him being inside his mother's womb, he might have a small chance of survival. His curiously furless, limp body would only accept the tiniest of sips. Soon, it became apparent a feeding tube was necessary, so great care had to be taken that I didn't overfeed him. After a week, his eyes started to glaze over, and I was struck with the realisation that he was going blind. His body was starting to stiffen up, and there was a coldness to him that made me realise I was only prolonging his suffering. By the end of the day, he was completely blind. I laid his head in my lap and gently stroked him. I knew what had to be done.

I went to Barry and asked that he be put out of his misery because, for the first time, I realised he was suffering, and it was only my stubborn pride that wouldn't let him go. Barry went off to do the hapless deed (but I suspect he hates putting animals down just as much as me), and he came back suggesting I give him one more day. I knew it was pointless, but I decided to bombard Calf with everything I had at my disposal to see if it would help. I went armed with a massive dose of cow penicillin and some fresh colostrum milk and administered both.

The next morning, fearing the inevitable, I went to the calf shed and there, stood in the corner, was the forlorn figure of the tiniest bull calf, trembling slightly, bald except for small sprouts of fur around the face. Just standing there, as though to prove something to us. The glazed coating over the eyes still remained, but he instinctively moved his head when I approached and nuzzled me, vulnerable, a fighter, and so in need of tender loving care. I felt spurred into action. He would be given as much colostrum milk as his little stomach could handle. I had calculated he should still have been in his mother's womb for another two months.

From then on, Calf turned an imaginary corner and he grew and grew and grew. His fur started to sprout over his body, too, and soon, he had the familiar black-and-white markings of a Friesian bull calf. The milky covering across his eyes eventually disappeared, and he was able to stand constantly at feeding times. But he was still "the ugliest creature to ever grace the earth", as the farm hands used to say when they would pop in to check on his progress. To me, he was just Calf. I looked past the misshapen face, the prematurity that seemed to be permanently etched upon him. In my eyes, he had obtained the greatest measure of beauty because of his will to survive.

As the months wore on, I decided to let him out of the calf pen to join me when I was in the garden. He became my gardening companion and, often, while I was silently weeding away, he'd just sit by me in mute companionship. With the onset of spring, occasionally he'd kick up his heels and race round and round the lawn pig-jumping as what I took to be his version of the one-fingered salute at all the nay-sayers. But his greatest pleasure was simply sniffing flowers of any kind. He would take a big sniff of a flower or bush that would take his fancy, then sniff the air as though committing that particular smell to memory. On one such occasion, he escaped the calf pen and I found him out in the garden with the remnants of some bloom he'd massacred stuck on his left nostril. I saw the beautiful rose petal stuck to that ugly bull-like nostril and, from then on, he became known as Ferdinand the Bull.

John the farm owner purchased all the bull calves from us as weaners and when the time came for Ferdinand to be lined up for purchase, John shook his head violently. "Uh-uh; no way, Susan. He's just too darn ugly. There's a retarded look about him, and even I have standards!"

I looked from Ferdinand to John, and I desperately wanted Ferdinand to take his place amongst his brethren. "Well now, John, ugly or not, he's all bull, so what I think is needed here is a little negotiation."

A deal was done, and Ferdinand became a fixture in the grazing paddocks. He also made up for lost time and grew into a colossus. All I had to do was call out his name and then I'd hear the thundering of hoofs and then a screech as he'd stop plum in front of me. I'd give that big ugly head a scratch, and then he'd give his signature sniff of the air around him before taking his place back with the boys.

I always knew Ferdinand was destined for the meatworks and this carried the air of inevitability that could not be denied. All too soon, it was his turn, and I said my goodbyes the day before. Taking the best bloom from the garden, I offered it to him, reminiscent of the last meal on death row, and I felt anger that this wonderful, rare beast had survived so many odds only to suffer such a common fate. He put his big ugly brute of a head against me, and I calmly patted it one last time.

Except Ferdinand was never loaded onto the truck the next day. I heard through the boys that he had injured his hip in an uncharacteristic display of unruliness. He simply couldn't be loaded. That evening, John happened to walk past me, and I couldn't hold back. "And you thought Ferdinand was retarded. I'd say what you have there is one very intelligent bull."

"Looks like." He gave a wry smile back.

Ferdinand saw out his days as the teaser bull for the milking herd, and to me, his beauty transcended the grotesqueness of that distorted bull head. I think all he ever wanted was to survive, and survive he surely did.

# Fistfuls of Mud

Little boy crouched over the puddle with such innocent delight,
Do you capture your reflection as your pretend friend?
Feel the worms squirm, clutching dreams with fistfuls of mud?
Hold on to them with two chubby little hands,
Because who knows what your grown-up future brings?
The rise to a glorious chorus of love?
Falling to the muted sepia strains of despair?
Perhaps rage about being boxed, stamped, despatched
By nameless, headless people?
Maybe to surrender your soul, only to take it back again?
Even taste that mystical last kiss of death?
But as a child, time hesitates, to become an endless stream of summers.

# For Bella

Little one, you're slipping away,
Your sharp bones silhouette in harsh relief,
Contrasting with your beautiful big brown eyes.
So soft are your eyes when you speak of love
For a mama stolen away at such a young age.
Her absence fills you with a hollow empty void
That leads you to despise your reflected self.
But hear your mama's words, Bella, as she looks down
From a place where beautiful mothers go
When their time on earth is complete.
"Do not cry, my child," she says each day.
"I am the gentle spirit that walks by your side,
I am the mother that wraps warm arms around you
When I hear your desperate pleas for help.
I am the one that softly kisses your cheek
To wipe the sad tears from your eyes.
I am your mama that wants you to get well
So we can all once again cherish your vibrant bright smile."

In the end, you willed your body and spirit to join her instead.

# Gardener's Delight

The anticipation is immense.
Drawn, the moth to the flame.
Strip off the corporate uniform
Slowly, savour the moment,
Get down and dirty.
Feel the earth curl round your fingers.
The sun engulf your body
As energy flows.

Weeds extracted
Expose what is
A perfect yellow rose,
Majestic in its glory.
The rhythm is set,
Time to chill,
Let the mind explore,
Salve to the soul,
All at once at peace
With honest toil.

# For Papa—A Lament

Two sides of a coin.
The body, facedown, exists barely,
Drawing in the final breaths
For what seems an eternity.
Your heart beats faintly,
Suffering eats time away slowly.
You lie in such stillness,
Lest some movement tilts the balance.

But turn the coin face up.
Your mind has become your fortress,
Where resistance reigns supreme.
A siege where the mind
Supersedes your body of works.
Your spirit blackens with the torment
Of a mind and body torn apart.
Let the two sides merge as one
To walk in peace through the beckoning gates
To make that final journey.

# Give It Your Best Shot

Death lurks in the corner of rooms,
On the sidewalks, in skyscrapers, on the killing fields,
Under the beds of the elderly and in the cots of very young.
You go about your deadly business silently, a determined,
cold-blooded assassin.
Ever-present, a musky, rotten, sweet smell that swirls,
curls, dances hypnotically
And drapes around the minds of even the bravest of women and men.

Your weapon is a sheet of ebony silk, a swathe of beauty worn in
collusion with the illusory gods of worship
That twists and turns as a serpent's black tongue,
constricting the life force,
Suffocating the free spirit until the charismatic false gods and you
Bring the people mercilessly and submissively to their knees.

Tell me your thoughts, Death, so clinically disembodied.
Do you ever hesitate, see your target in the scope and then drift on by?
No, you go about your day-to-day duties which great gusto, I think,
And wage a determined war against open minds,
feasting on their insecurities.

I know a wrought woman who is stamped with your decay.
She carries a megawatt smile on her face
Then you can see the lights suddenly switch off
As her thoughts cast back to acknowledge you.
The sadness in her eyes as they look away
Into a vista of regret, dread, and heartbreak.

I know a wrought man who's as strong as an ox.
He can fight three men with one hand tied behind his back,
But he cowers and quivers at the mere mention of your name.
A big, tough guy who can be felled with one five-letter word,
Such is your powerful all-consuming influence.

# Glory Days

Marble champion for almost a year,
Glint of steel in my eyes,
Ruthless in my intent
To take on the Beasley Block Boys.
My ultimate challenge is won,
Achieving muted boyish respect.

A menagerie of pets,
Bringing home all the local strays,
Made a doghouse for Kandy she never slept in.
Magpie continually threatening to dethrone the cat.
Rushing home from school,
Cold winter days,
Homemade pea and ham soup bubbling on the stove.
Sweet smell of cookies cooling on the trays,
Mum—the Pied Piper calling the tune.
Wafting aromas draw the neighbourhood kids in.

Sledging down the Sugarloaf,
All guts and pride,
Heart pounding so loudly,
Bumps threaten to unseat my ride.
Must save face or risk ridicule,
So I cling on for dear life.
Gave CPR to the sole surviving guinea pig;
Vivid recollection of Mum's exasperated face.

Sunday drives to the local wineries,
Dad desperate for his weekly grog.
Sneak wine tastes when the monks turn their backs,
Arrive home giggly,
Much to Mum's disgust!

Happy days,
Glory days,
Children running free.
Only the best memories remembered
In human nature's defence,
As it should always be.

# Groundhog Day

My son came home from war today,
Just 22 years of age,
A non-combatant engineer
In service for the country he loved.

Traditional battlefields weren't drawn;
Urban warfare in all its dangerous deceit.
A bloody turmoil of despair,
Tears spilt in the ghettos and streets.

This is Iraq's filthy war,
Based on a dirty lie.
A son completing the work a father left undone
In the name of world peace.

My son fought in zealous pursuit
Of all we hold true and fair.
Except no one told him
The truth was never there.

Anger turns to violence
As realism filters through.
An emperor exposed for the clothes never worn.
He's opened a Pandora's box.

A poor country, rich in resource,
Caught in a battle for control,
Raped time and time again;
Our countries play a pivotal role.

An illusion that becomes a truism
Built on a foundation of sand.
It shifts and slides from side to side;
A war that can never be won.

My son came home from war today
In a makeshift coffin with a flag draped across.
A hero, with a body torn to shreds;
Please tell me to what purpose.

# Rainbow With Black as a Shadow

Blue–Green collide
Translucent Turquoise
Calm or storm
Calm before the storm, perhaps?
Kaleidoscope of colours...
Yellow; celestial lights
Magenta; loving colour
Pink; the colour of lies
Midnight blue; the colour of my truth
Red; judgement day
Black; the shadow of impending death
*"Here's looking at you kid!"*

# Heartland

Your exquisite grasslands tapestry,
Boundless mountainous beauty.
Endless clouds
Interspersed with
Azure skies
A striking backdrop to
Emerald green.
Feel the wind,
Taste the sea,
Touch the earth,
Hear my language spoken.
Your soul reaches out,
I have rebuilt,
I will return soon.

# Home at War

When do we stop viewing
the world like a child?
When do we lose
the wonder, the awe
Looking At, With, In, To
The urge to explore.
Do we wake up one day
And just blindly say, "This is the time
When all frightfully serious
Thingies take place"?
Work is a chore,
People are a bore,
Children to rear,
Society to bear,
Bills to pay,
Passion dissipates,
But Time still moves on,
And before we know it,
Our Wonderland and World is gone.

# Hope is that intangible thing

It's standing on top of a hillside and feeling the breeze lift your spirit skyward to soar with the silhouette of birds in their flight.

It's walking down the street and believing that a solemn stranger is giving you a slight smile in return.

It's the lone piper on the hill, where the strains of his wistful notes echo in perfect symphony with the rhythmic concerto of his beating heart.

It's the otter playfully tumbling and turning in her sparking river playground, oblivious to the efforts to keep her species alive.

It's the hope that lives inside of an unborn child and the belief that she will carry her serious message forward to a new hopeful world.

# I am glass

I am glass.
See me shatter
Into a kaleidoscope of threads
Too small to capture the light.
Watch with horrific fascination
As I hit the wall,
This immovable obstacle
Met full-on
With stubborn determination.

I am glass.
Watch me smash then fall
In the slow motion
Of a head on collision.
Touch the shafts of glass
As I dissipate
Plastered against the wall.

I was glass.
Now I'm stuck to the wall.
In essence, I've lost my true form;
I'm nothing at all.
Will all the kings men
Put me together again?
No, I will.

# In Defence of the Middle-Aged Woman in Baudelaire's "Windows" Portrait

I see you across the rooftops,
A man stood in sullen silence.
Yet you look upon me intently;
Shall I shake you from your reverie?
Shall I intrude into your world, ever so slightly?
Piece by piece, moment by moment,
Stripping back the bare cliché
No doubt attributed to me.
Shall I give you my blue-sky view?
Crossing back and forth between the shadows of illusion and reality,
Or my monochrome snippets in strict focus,
Leaving aside other false virtues.
How convenient distance is for you;
You make it your treasured friend.
Yet why not just a mutual acquaintance?
I held your eyes once,
And I felt your feelings,
Weighed them up in the palm of my hand.
Then released them,
Because I too was afraid.
Ah, perhaps you think I stoop from middle-age
And the weight of irreconciled fantasies,
When indeed I stoop to reflect you;
Is that so hard to comprehend?
I could stand at the window,

# Transparent Moments

Resplendent in my fine gossamer gown,
Transparent with need to connect with you,
Then you'd see beyond your skim-the-surface peeping
The lustre of a woman beyond need,
A creature of passion, or is that desire?
Possessed by a savage basic instinct
To merge as one with a fellow being.
If you became my lover, could I bear to let you go?
Would you place a glaze around my heart?
The sweet taste of fulfilment, then regret,
So I would be then forced to eat away
At your carefully composed stance.
There is no glory in mutual grief,
Just a curious empty defeat.
Therefore, man of intrepid mystery, who views upon me,
Do not feel pity for such as me,
For I may then be forced to pity such as you.

# Fear Not

I do not fear the passions that rage inside me.
They are the thrill, the ride, the essence of me.

I do not fear the silence of my home.
My inner voice whispers to the walls and
Seeps under the doorway to the world beckoning.

I do not fear nature in her majestic glory.
She provides the wrath, the rapture,
That exquisite crystalline beauty that encompasses all.

I do not fear the corporate hyenas in their pin-striped suits.
They gorge off the underbelly of society and then devour each other.

I do not fear technology. I know it well enough to see its susceptibility
To all the faults and misconceptions that its creators have in abundance.

I do not fear death. I've felt the serenity that embraces you
When you glimpse the white light that leads I know not where.

What I do fear is ridicule for my artistic endeavours
Without rhyme, reason, or regard.

# Dad

I got to organise your funeral on Thursday. They rang me at 6 am. I didn't even get to answer the call. I promised you I would be there at the end to hold your hand, but you bloody went and died without telling me. I will not cry. If I cry, it means you have hurt me. Instead, I will rest my tears in the pit of my stomach, let them settle awhile, then let them slowly rise, infiltrate my lungs, and manoeuvre their way up through my throat until I taste the salt of my grieving. I gave you my word that you would not die alone. I will remain mute and decide if guilt should enter into the reality of your death.

I quibble over small details. The sloppy joes and trackpants, new, sitting in a bag in my room, the ones I failed to deliver last week, using the excuse that you had the time to spare. When did time slow for you? Pyjamas had been your uniform for a while. I guess I equated them with illness rather than your agedness. Clothes were meant to lift you somehow. Now I dawdle over your burial clothes, query the idea of a suit, a salute to formality. But there is no passing up this event. It's your assigned time to leave this earth, today at 1 pm.

And, in some perverse way, I'm going to miss my visits to the nursing home. Sometimes, you could be so sweet but sometimes, it was hard to love you. It's got to be better than pity—right? Pity is a deceptive emotion, layers upon layers of malignant subterfuge. Christ, who are we both kidding? "I" figured prominently in your life and when you ran out of "I"s to use, you replaced them with a "me" instead. But in a lot of ways, you yearned for freedom, and it was hard for you to be tied down with a wife and large family.

I still remember the sandals you brought back from Mexico. They had little colourful flowers on the toes. They were fun and different. You could be like that sometimes. Or the time we were sitting in a Toledo restaurant; you were having a heart attack. I got you to drink red wine. I didn't know the word for hospital in Spanish. You took my hand to still my fear. You could be so brave.

But in life, loneliness in the dying process was your greatest fear. You could say the people around you turned away a long time ago. You fed your isolation while they feasted on it. A small boy, afraid to come out from under the table. We never took the time to understand. It was just your way of dealing with things. So, Dad, it goes something like this: death is the plain and simple truth. It's the living that provides for all the perceptions and reflections. And you know, Dad, you lived how you died. A little afraid but always the fighter until the end. I just wished I could have been there to hold your hand.

# I am Woman (To Mum)

Clear, hazel eyes,
Sofia Loren-like cheekbones,
Wide, generous mouth,
Vivacious, courageous,
Ageless beauty within.

Housewife in the '50s,
Devotional slave to society.
Three breakdowns;
Never broke down.

Strength in spirit,
Defying all odds,
Fighting the curse of booze
Infiltrating your live.

Married in purgatory
For 35 years.
Left him one day and started anew.
Took your unshakeable belief with you.

Placed on a pedestal
You've never come down from.
The ultimate survivor:
Woman, mother, and friend.

# If I ...

If I should ever murmur my thoughts and fears,
Please know it means I have finally rejected
All sensible concept and succumbed
To the emotional rebellion within my heart.

If I should sigh your name with hesitance,
Alone, on a windswept shore and feel it
Lifted by the whimsical breeze, know I'll
Drift with my timid words to find you.

If I should see your face in the haze
Of the half-wakened state of my dreamtime,
Know I will gently stroke it, place a
Finger to your lips in a soft stolen kiss.

If I should ever feel your pain,
Such as the pain you feel in silent moments,
Be consoled that two compressed souls
May merge into the fragile tapestry of being.

If I should ever put these feelings to verse,
Know it's purely this—I desire your beautiful heart.

## The Death of a Fawn and the Canvas Created

I will not say you are a pretty sight.
On the tillered land you did fall,
Perhaps at the end of a hunter's gun?
But there is, none the less, a still dignity about you
As you superimpose yourself on the ground.
Of course, decomposition has lent its hand;
Decay will create its own mottled parchment
Of cream, fawn, brown and rotting flesh,
A canvas that nature now bows down to.
You are worthy of that moment's pause,
To know you did not cower in death,
Creature of grace, fleet of foot, and youthful startled energy.

# Impressions of Insanity— up close and personal

The sands of time move through our minds
As we suffer the swings of outrageous fortune.
We are the cerebrally wounded walking through the fog,
Medicated to bring clearness back from self-exile.
Can clarity be achieved when the mind is so clouded?
Can the lost come back to the fold
When the bridge lies as a ramshackle testament
To the destructive nature of man's human side?

# Joy—A Lament

She was born at a time when the moon was high and the beams
pierced through to the hospital room.
They all looked on with awe as she gave them the most exquisite smile.
The young mother gave her a fierce hug, but she knew that love
would quickly turn to hate with the memories of how she'd been
forcefully conceived.
So she named her Joy and gave her up to the state.

The state duly complied and sent her to a foster home.
As the months followed, the baby didn't utter a cry.
The foster father declared her "not right" and it was with great
sorrow the foster mum delivered her back to the state.
Joy only smiled!

The state then sent her to an orphanage run by an order of strict nuns.
At two, Joy wanted to play; they wanted her to learn to pray.
So, they declared her possessed by the devil, brought an exorcist in to
cleanse her soul, and it failed miserably, so back to the state she went.
Joy only smiled!

All in a dither, the state consigned her over to the scientists
interested in bottling her special thing.
So, they poked and prodded, took numerous tubes of blood, sat
glued to their microscopes.
Joy happily played with the animals in the science labs and, by the time
she was nine, they accepted no hypothesis could explain her uniqueness.

So, they turned her over to the psychologists to try their luck.
Joy only smiled!

The psychologists tried a more subtle approach. They simply
observed, night and day, through the years … They painstakingly
documented then debated every possible conceptual nuance.
Joy sat quietly and read as many books as she could.
Upon finding no suitable explanation, the psychologists returned
her to the real world.
Joy only smiled!

Then a businessman came up with a commercial proposition.
He'd use her face and megawatt smile to sell things.
So, she appeared on billboards, television, and magazines,
Until the businessman decided he wanted a bit of Joy himself.
Suffering shock, she took her money and ran as far as she could.
She suddenly stopped smiling!

Then deep sorrow reflected in her eyes as she realised
She'd been screwed by the state,
The nuns had tried to screw with her spirit,
The scientists had tried to screw with her body,
The psychologists had tried to screw with her mind,
And the businessman just screwed her over completely.
As she patted her swelling belly, she knew the cycle must end.
And as the beams of light touched her face,
Joy went away permanently.

# Joy

It can catch you
In the car, a bus, across a crowded room.
A feeling of wellness,
A feeling of just being.

For one brief moment,
Captured in panoramic vision,
The clouds disperse.
A kaleidoscope of colour filters through,
A crescendo to the last movement,
The conductor brings his baton down,
Caught in symphonic grace
Inside your head.

# Judgement

Do not try to judge what cannot be judged.
Do you question the misshapen bill of the platypus?
The wildflower that incongruously appears in a crack on the sidewalk?
The mysterious and haunting etherealness of the autistic child?
The spider offspring that feasts off the carcass of its mother?
The honeybee's one sting that renders it lifeless?
The tiny soldier ant that carries a load many times its own weight?
The seeking of that small patch of insipid sunlight on a bleak foggy morn?
The turmoil of the soul, the flow of essential lifeblood through the veins,
Seemingly unquenchable against the still heat of the night?
I ask you this question because I want you to consider
Some things are because they just simply are;
Reason against thought, illusion versus reality,
Rage against serenity, disorder versus harmony.
Once again, I ask you because I want you to consider
Some things just are, as they are intended to be;
Somewhere in there, there's a place for me.

# Kafka, Me, and Bobby McGee

I'll wrap it up a lot tighter this time
In thorns and barbed wire.
Make it impenetrable
Against beautiful, meaningless words,
Suspicious siren songs,
Passionate pretend images.
Heard it all before, me and Bobby McGee!

I'm not a grey mouse to be toyed with
Dangled from a shabby piece of string.
Reeled out at your pleasure,
Let loose when I'm to perform.
Cheshire cat, concubine convenor,
One trick pony without a rider
Bent on mindless destructive delight.

So, take your loss on the chin,
Don't call out to me
In moments when you ache for destiny.
The cupboard is bare;
I need to feed my life.
Don't you need to sustain yours?
Even Dionysus knew about hope.

Stone man with your stone heart;
Heavy hand of fate.
Bring on all the philosophy,
Literature you can lay your hands on.
My reclusive Kafka,
Sitting in your dark tower,
Turning your mind away from the light.

# Kate

They called her Crazy Kate,
Where lunacy sat well.
Rolling eyes, frothing mouth,
Confirmed hater of men
Forced into service of the land.

They called her Crazy Kate,
She of indeterminable age,
A slickness of body, independence of spirit,
Where madness had its rewards.

I called her just Kate.
Soft mouth, with reins held loose,
I passed her tough friendship test;
Oh, flighty lady, who taught me to ride.

I called her my Kate.
A bond built between friends.
This trusted companion,
Confessor to my sins,
Always silent of the subject;
Unconditional love returned.

I called this horse Kate,
And released her back to the wilds
When age had overtaken her,
To wander free again.

*Service provided in full.*

# My friend Kate

I had a friend once, a special friend who came to me just when I needed her most. I remember the first day I saw her. She was a wild chestnut mare, left to languish up in the hills because she was considered too crazy to ride. The talk roundabouts was that her mother was named "Crazy Kate" because no-one could stick long enough in the saddle to say they had actually ridden her, and she had passed on the mantle to her highly strung daughter.

As a prank on me, four shepherds had brought her down into the yards. I squinted in the midday sun as I saw her coat was disturbed with the white froth of exertion and her eyes were rolled like a madwoman trapped by the fear that only being confined can bring. I instinctively knew she pranced up and down sizing up the height of the railings in a bid for her freedom once again. There was no grass in the yards, no huge hill to peer out from or survey her domain as only the regal do. Yes, she was regal, not so much in her look—she was quarter horse crossed with farm hack, only 14.2 hands, an ordinary chestnut mare, really, that'd been forgotten up in the hills until her call for servitude had been ordained. It was more the way she held herself—her bearing, if you like. If I had to pinpoint it, I would have to say, it was the set of her head and neck, the height of her tail, and that indefinable quality that only the truly noble have.

I stood at a distance from the yards and felt an involuntary smile come at the look of disdain she issued the four shepherds it had taken to run her into the ground. I'm sure if she could have spat at their feet, she would have.

"Hey, Sue, you wanted a horse to ride—here she is!" I felt like a dog being called to heel. Aren't all female dogs called Sue? They all turned in my direction, a gleam in their eyes and a quick involuntary exchange of snide glances as they contemplated what would happen next. I wiped my hands on my jeans, as though I was set to get down to business, and then paused, giving them a feigned look of complete innocence.

"Nah—you guys have a go first; she looks really green to me." I'd issued the challenge, laid down the gauntlet, and waited expectantly for that inevitable measure of pride to break in at least one of them.

Roscoe, the "Rasta rider", went first. He was considered the most cavalier amongst them. "Here, give me the saddle. I'll teach this mad bitch a thing or two."

I watched her coat ripple in nervous waves as she felt the unfamiliar weight of the blanket and saddle go on her back. Every now and then, she would turn her head, judging the progress being made, yet she stood perfectly still, with a calmness that almost defied belief. They forced a halter over her head. It had seen years of use and had crude pieces of rope attached to it to act as reins. There was no gentleness in their touch, only a lust to prove something.

Was it dominance in general, or just a desire to pit themselves against a stray horse whose reputation for madness had preceded her? Man versus beast—the cliché that had gone on since time and memorial.

He jumped on with his bowed legs, cockiness, and the ease of a rider who'd spent years in the saddle. I started counting in my head. I was surprised I got to twelve before he was flung several feet into the air and unceremoniously dumped on his butt.

He wiped himself off and mumbled, "Jeez, I guess she's greener than I thought."

Then the next one tried, and the next, until pretty soon, they were all dusting themselves off, awash with ill-concealed pride. The look of disdain she gave them was well worth the comedy show. I walked up to her, looked her square in the eyes, and smiled with my hands, smiled with soft words, smiled at her rebellious individualism. The tremors I felt were of real fear, a brave fear that was wasted on the pitifully small audience gathered.

I silently wished for a miracle and, feeling just as shaky myself, I got one of the lads to give me a leg up, and before I knew, it I was sat plum in the saddle. Both of us seemed to pause and wait then for the inevitable to happen. But it didn't. Whether she was just plain tuckered out from all her exertions or she felt my tremors and took pity on me, I still don't know to this day, but when I took my heart in my mouth and edged her forward, there were no horsy acrobatics, just a calm, sedate walk. Round and round we walked in the yards, clockwise then anti-clockwise, and so engrossed were we that I didn't even register the shepherds fade away, disappointed they weren't going to see me bite the dirt as well.

I moved her into the paddock near the house. I wanted her to feel my closeness. I wanted to tempt her with treats; carrots and meal became her favourites. Was it easy catching her the next day and the next or even the day after that? No, it wasn't. She would strut around the paddock in a show of wonderful independence and only allow me to saddle her up when she was ready. I knew the score; it was her way or the highway, and yet, initially, it had to be that way. Sometimes, I would just stand there with tears in my eyes, with the complete frustration of watching her playfully trot round, never too far but never close enough. But whether she'd sense that I was about at the end of my tether, I don't know. Invariably, she would stop in front of me and nudge my hand forward as if to say, "Well, come on then; get on with it!"

Before long, I'd rush home from work and imagine this would be the day that I could truly say we were a team. Oh, how wrong I was! The number of times I cursed her because I was late feeding the calves or late getting tea ready were just too numerous to contemplate. But there was no going back; she was too much of a challenge to walk away from. And sometimes, if I was really running late, I'd just wait for her to come over to me and talk about the day I'd had, spill out my woes and stroke her head, neck, and mane or simply brush her down. Every now and then, I'd see her eyes almost close, as though she was simply comforted by a stray human touch somehow.

Initially, our riding was confined to the house paddock, but gradually, as I gained confidence, I was able to take her to the longer dairy paddocks. She gave me no quarter at all. She knew only two speeds: trot and gallop. There was certainly no in-between for her.

My natural inclination was to pull heavily on her mouth, out of fear more than anything else. Of course, this would get her hackles up, and I could feel her fight the bit, shaking her head vigorously as if to show me there was a better way.

On one of our excursions, I held genuine fear for my safety. I envisaged falling off and breaking my neck because of my inability to control her bursts of speed. I got to the gate, my arm muscles complaining bitterly, and Callum, the head shepherd, was waiting for us.

"Ya know she really likes you, don't you?"

"Yeah, right—she's got a funny way of showing it," I mumbled in disappointment.

"Ya know what your problem is, don't ya?"

"Please tell me, because I'm running out of ideas," I almost pleaded.

"Ya sawing on her mouth. Ya hurting her when ya pull on the reins so hard. She's got a fair dinkum soft mouth, and every time ya pull hard, she'll fight ya all the way!" He reached over to pat her and she flinched.

"You reckon?" I started to feel guilty about my ignorance.

"Yeah, sure thing, kid. It's a dead cert. Ya can hang in the saddle fine, but loosen the reins and use your legs more, and she'll stop playing up, okay?"

"Sure, I'll give it a go. What's there to lose except my dignity if she turfs me?" I reasoned out loud.

"Yep—and don't forget, a good stockhorse is ridden every day, and never gallop her downhill, right? Jeez—Crazy Kate. I never thought I'd see the day when she'd let someone ride her." He walked down the race, shaking his head.

"Sure, I'll remember that!" I yelled out after him. I felt a burst of happiness then. I was just pleased he considered that she was going to make a good stockhorse.

Things improved immeasurably after that. Through trial and error, sometimes more trial than error, I learnt to use the pressure of my legs to guide her. She noticed it, too. I fancied, during this time, she'd turn her head and give a silent acknowledgement that I was finally learning.

Summer holidays became magical. With no classes to teach, I was able to spend more time on the station with her and the real work began for us. We'd be sent to take dry cows, in-calf heifers, and yearlings to and from the hills out the back, past the Papua flats. I fancied I was a real cowboy then, just me and my trusty steed, at one with the world in general. It was hard work but good work, and I could feel muscles developing that I never knew existed before. There was no greater feeling than being on top of the highest hilltop looking out on a warm summer's day with a slight coastal breeze gently cooling us. We were simply masters of all we surveyed.

    Kate enjoyed it, but she seemed to reserve special delight for drafting. I truly believe it was what she was bred for. Even when the task looked insurmountable, I'd point her to a cow, and she'd intuitively know which direction to take and swerve and move so that it would be cut from the rest. I quickly figured out that all I had to do was hang on and she'd do the rest. There was never an animal that beat her. Even when we were called upon to draft from a particularly feisty gathering of two-year old bulls, she'd just put her head down and lunge forward with all the strength of a locomotive and yet turn with the grace of a ballerina. She could turn on a sixpence and she'd never let up until the job was done.

    I remember a couple of the shepherds just happen to watch us hard at work one day, and afterwards, they trotted up and one of them said rather bashfully, "Gee, you can sure ride."

    I looked at him intently and said, "No, I hang on; it's Kate here that makes me look good," and gave her sweaty neck a big hug.

    They swung away then, but I think it gave them something to think about beyond counting sheep.

    Every now and then, Kate would become beset with naughtiness. I think the last bastion of her test she'd set for me was to see me flat-out on the ground with her looking down at me with a horse face of goofy delight. And her biggest attempt came about a year into our friendship. This happened when we were galloping across the sands of "Papua One" without a care in the world. That was until she went from full gallop to a sudden stop. She just put on all the anchors as she got it in her head to have a roll in the sand. She knelt down and was all set for the big roll when I gave her a hefty kick in the side and yelled, "What the hell, Kate? I'm still on your back!"

She looked round then as though genuinely surprised that I was still in situ and then calmly got back on to all fours and we continued on our way as though nothing had happened. But something did happen that day. Maybe she simply accepted that I'd always stick to her like glue, or perhaps it registered that she could have genuinely hurt me. I don't know; all I know is she never pulled a stunt like that again.

Kate really came into her own the day an unforecast cyclone hit the area. It was so unseasonal and so unexpected. It hit with a ferocity and power that caught us off guard completely. We'd been nine months in continuous drought, so initially, the driving rain and wind were greeted with delight.

Before we knew it, the lower paddocks were under water and the cowshed was rendered almost useless. I couldn't get to work; being eight months pregnant, my days had been cut down considerably, anyway. The roads were all closed, and the boys worked with their motorbikes to get the milking cows and young stock to higher ground and to relative safety.

That left the in-calf heifers and springing cows. Baz came in with a worried look on his face. The motorbikes simply couldn't handle the water that had built up in the low-lying areas. I volunteered our services. He said flat-out, "No," but I pushed on regardless. I knew Kate would look after me; she had slowed down considerably in the past months, I think out of silent regard for my condition.

As luck would have it, the wind dropped considerably, but the rain still hung in there unabated. I remember thinking, *This is what the eye of a storm must feel like*, as, draped in oilskins and plastered with huge drops of rain, we slowly, bit by bit, edged the heavily pregnant stock to higher ground. Every now and then, Kate would look back at me and I would say, "It's okay, girl; let's keep moving." I knew we'd be out of the eye of the storm soon enough, so it was important to get as much done as possible in the time we had left.

Eventually, the job was complete. We didn't stop until every animal was deposited in a safe new paddock out of harm's way. We slowly ambled back to the relative warmth of the house. Kate was put in a secure paddock to see out the storm, and I retired inside, the pangs of pre-mature labour pains starting quite ominously. Through all the drama that occurred soon after, I kept thinking to myself, *Only a horse and rider could have done what we did.* Machinery had been rendered useless when it was really needed the most.

Finally, fate stepped in; doesn't it always? We were told the owner's son wanted to take over looking after the dairy herd and stock. We accepted it with quiet resignation and, as luck would have it, managed to procure a better position across the country. It also meant organising to take Kate with us. I never stopped to think that she couldn't be floated. I automatically assumed that our bond was so strong that she'd follow me to the ends of the earth if I asked her to. I asked permission from the station owner, John, to take her with us.

A look of ill-disguised guilt came across his face.

"I've heard it told she's been your horse since the day you hopped on her—of course you can take her; you'd be doing me a favour, actually."

I walked away with a spring in my step. My plans were falling all into place: a new farm, a new baby, and a new life.

By leaving day, we'd got everything ready for the big shift. It was planned that Kate would be floated last.

A few of the station folk had assembled as a last hurrah, and I brought Kate up among the small throng to lead her into the compact metal float. She arced up the moment she saw it. I thought it was just a temporary thing. I talked to her continuously, egging her on, cajoling her to go up the ramp.

Eventually, after several aborted efforts, she did quietly walk up into the body of the float. Then all hell broke loose as I went to secure her. She lashed out, delirious with the surroundings and smashing her body against anything she could in violent protest.

In that instant, amongst the gloom of the horse float, I saw Kate's rolling eyes, I felt the sweat of terror, I heard her shrieks of anguish and was instantly transported back to three years prior, when a stray horse with attitude, a rough-hewn coat, and a look of stark fear had graced the yards. I felt a knot in my throat constrict and almost gag my windpipe, and I knew I'd do anything to stop the pounding of her legs wildly against the metal sides. I pushed her back then as quickly as I could, out into the sunlight, out of her forced enclosure.

Baz quietly asked, "Do you realise your hand is bleeding?"

"No, is it?" I said automatically.

I heard his words, but I watched Kate, almost mesmerised, as a wave of calmness seemed to wash over. She became still, so still and she just looked at me then with those kind big brown eyes, simply asking me to do the right thing by her.

"Jeez, I really thought she'd go in for you, but I guess if the madness is there, it's always there, right?" Kevin the farmhand said.

I ignored his crass comment, instead looking directly at the farm owner, who had come over to say his goodbyes, and quietly asked, "If I take her out the back, will you promise me she can roam the hills and see out her days?"

"Sure; you have my word on that."

That was good enough for me. John was a man of his word, and I knew he'd honour it.

"You'd better see to your hand; your finger is looking mangled," Baz reminded me.

I walked around Kate, softly stroking her coat, inspecting the damage I'd inadvertently inflicted on her. There were a few spots of blood, some minor scratches, but nothing that would stop me doing what I knew I had to do.

We were a sombre walking party that afternoon, Kate, Baz, and I, as we headed quietly, methodically, out beyond the blue gums, across the Papuas, and ending up at the foot of the hills.

My finger throbbed like hell, and it appeared to be at a crooked angle, but I placed my arms round her neck and gave her the biggest hug I could muster. I quickly took off the halter, her symbol of servitude, I guess, and stepped back, waiting for the inevitable. She stood there and looked at me then, just for a couple of seconds longer than normal, and I said goodbye in my mind; I fancied she was doing the same back. She turned then and smoothly trotted towards the incline as though she was putting on one last glorious show for me, a show of grace, a show of beauty, where a noble spirit was returning from whence she had come. I didn't cry during this time; I forced my eyes to remain clear as I watched her depart my life.

As Baz and I walked back in companionable silence ready for the big move to another town, a new beginning, I looked at him and saw there was a dab of moisture in his eyes.

"You know," he said in that quiet, gruff way he had, "that horse sure loved you."

"Yes, I know."

To this day, in a still moment, I look at the crooked index finger of my right hand and I fancy I can see a small chestnut mare up on the highest hilltop looking out to the sea, a beautiful crazy mare who taught me how to ride, who simply brought so much joy to my life.

# Kookaburra Calling

O Kookaburra, high up on the telegraph pole,
One eye on the world, one eye on me,
Regal in your survey and stillness,
What do you see when you look down on me?

Do you see my eyes look to the sky,
Filled with winged envy?
The air an unconquerable citadel
Thats parts him from me.

In my reverie, I hear your kookaburra cry,
A hoary cackle, your mournful communiqué,
Waiting for the echo from your mate,
Yet no correspondent call is returned.

Last night, Kookaburra, you appeared in my dream.
You spoke softly to me,
"Ah—but I'm not a bird, *ma chérie!*"
"What are you then?" I queried.
"I am the one you've been calling."

# Lake Song

Invisible hand,
Fingertips extend,
Guide me from the water
Bathed in moonlight dew.
Let me wash you anew,
Faceless forest master.
Feel my ripened lips
Whisper sweet enchantments,
Cast fragile spells
On your translucent skin.
How moist the potency of your body?
Dance slowly, with the sinuous sighs of the trees,
Join with the echoes of their sensation,
Sway, sensuous drumbeat.
Desire, oh glorious desire,
Pound loud, soft then loud,
Shadow, pulsation, illumination,
Voodoo trance.
Touch the essence
Of honeyed incursion,
Exquisite prelude,
Eyes wide open,
Body supine, tied.
*Odalık* captured by rapture.
Lured expectation
For one night only
To the leafy bed
Of primeval dance.

## Sweet Dreams

Little one, you clench my heart.
I feel your pain,
Let me cradle you in a sea of dreams,
Hold you close, so the waves of calmness crash over us.

I am your guide.
I am fortified.
Yet my eyes see your tears, my ears hear your cries,
I feel the burning of your brow.

I will hold you close,
Sing you a soft lullaby.
Take your pain,
Gently rock you to sleep.

*Dedicated to all the mums whose sons and daughters have gone to fight miserable wars—we are the forgotten ...*

# Letter to My Son

*Tell me what I don't know, son.* Help me understand why you must fight this wretched conflict in all its dangerous deceit. Please know this endless crusade is based on a despicable lie. With two prophets at war, we swoop in to destabilise more, a son yearning to complete the work a father left undone—protect the oil at all costs.

*Don't you see, son,* the white feathers of peace blow silently away from a land bogged down in sand, dust, mud, and slush. Primitive mud huts litter the ravaged landscape, but the seven types of takeaway joints dotted strategically around the army compound will shield you from all that. I even hear Taco Bell's moving in around June!

*You know, son*—the wheels of commerce still churn in the middle of a bloody war. They feed off the backs of soldiers' needs and, as they watch your bellies grow, they wring their hands with glee as the seeds of smug self-satisfaction set in. Don't become the gun-toting, rooting-tooting moronic parody of what a respected soldier should be.

*And this isn't a picnic, my boy,* this is a land where you are respected by what type of gun you carry; AKs are common place—but above all, the pistol demands respect. They follow the creed of "know not the man but the gun"—but surely if you know the man, then it's harder to use the gun!

*I plead with you, son*, do not treat the people of this once-noble land with disrespect. Help them rise up from the shards of religious discord and a raving despot. Play soccer with them, laugh with them—not at them, rejoice in their diverse culture, but keep one eye open to the dangers that lurk in every dark alley and shadowed corner.

*You grew from my womb, son*, and that bond of unconditional love will never break. But I rage inside, a gut-wrenching, impotent rage that you chose this way to live out your *Boy's Own* dream. I implore that the winds of war wash over you and leave you physically, emotionally, and spiritually intact.
*You are my son; march to the drums of peace.*

*Love, Mum xxx*

# Logs Stacked

Before you went, you said,
"It's good to replenish what is gone."
The logs stayed stacked,
The enduring fragrance of pine
Long since dead with the onset
Of a score of winter chills.
I saw you once, casually walking along the street,
Sparks of recognition banked down by a sense of calm.
I passed on by, this perfect stranger.
Eyes lit, focusing on the next corner.
The logs could stay stacked,
The fire could wait, the day burned bright.

# Losing Time

When did I last stop to smell the roses,
caught up in the hustle-bustle of life?
Time marches on, unrelenting, faster—faster ...
I look to the sky. "How can I make time work for me? Please help me."
"Not I," said the Sun. "When is it the last time you let my rays wash
over you, heal you?"
"Not I," said the Moon. "When did you last gaze upon me for light,
for inspiration?"
"Not I," said the Stars. "With my canopy of beauty,
you no longer view me with bright eyes."
So I plead, "Who will help me?"
"I will," said Time. "But you must stop fighting me."

# Lullaby

Sleep, my little one,
Go to a world where demons fear to tread.

Let me sing you a lullaby
Of hope, beauty, and renewal.

Let me use a cold compress
To cool the burning of your brow.

Let me soothe your sorrow
That arcs into me.

By gently cradling your body against mine,
I will take away the pain.

I am tired, too,
From this reflected ache that builds incessantly.

Close your eyes, my darling,
Sleep the sleep of the innocent ...

# Marathon Man

You are running your marathon.
Feet pounding, ankles jarring against
That pitted static surface sealing
Concrete, bitumen, and asphalt.
Hard, immobile, unforgiving,
Lest a mistake is made.
Picking yourself up again; propel forward
Motion, demotion, forging on against time.
Tick, tock, until the clock stops.
Constants of movement,
Dynamics, dramatics, progression,
See the boy in the crowd, grimy, grinning,
Dream-weaver, swirling innocence, hopeful, playful,
Wearing the face of your past, present, future.
Nothing stands stagnant, still, stationary.
The push; the continual pushing to your finish line.
The ghosts of your forefathers calling you,
The eagle soars, fly with him, breath in his spirit
As your lungs gasp short, rasping, halting breaths,
Gorge your oxygen-enriched blue-blood veins,
Overlay them with that essential cry of freedom.
Odin, mystical one-eye, all-seeing, all-feeling,
Hugin and Munin, clear the paths blotted with the dots
Of bystanders with their leery, hungry, insatiable appetites.
So you forge on, that taskmaster exhaustion gives you no respite,
The visions of lovers rain down on your parade,

The procession; demanding, inviting, mug shots of memories.
Ruby lips, brunette hues, your type, sweat covered bodies seeking satiety.
Seeking more—a piece of your running heart not on offer, perhaps?
Still they dance on, jiving to the morbid beat of your pounding feet.
Gods litter the road, the debris of that illusory one true god mixes with
The grime, paper, cigarette butts that lie dirty, discarded on the sidewalk.
But let me help lift you that one step further,
The elusive finish line where uncertainty may cloud the vision.
The body screams out for release, the red brick road winds never-ending.
Feel my strong arms comfort your pains, your quest in pursuit of perfection,
Cushion the lead weights of your running shoes,
heavy with the burdens of duty.
Feel that chemical natural high that only endurance
can give lift you, carry you on,
Cross that finish line, feel the pride, be humbled,
shout out the joy, it's now your time.
Let victory wash through you, around you, surround you,
the essence of you filled.
With the peace of mind of what is earned and
that only final recognition can give,
Let no man or woman take asunder.

# Masquerade

You told me life was a masquerade ball, and I believed you—I always do!

I sat with my distance and politely inquired, "What mask will you wear today?" You stood still, like stone, centred within your own auditorium ... I itched to capture your face, infuse it with vigour and light, but your prophet mask remained, a study in boredom and superiority.

I danced around you, making my pact with your devil, doing my sensitive citizen samba with a twist of sultry sway before taking my place at the side of the stage to watch you perform.

Last night I dreamed, with no apparent will to resist you, you wearing your husband, teacher, lover, party masks, all piled on top of each other. You said it gave dimension to your face, but I knew the truth—the wife, child, mistress, party, all demanded they stay firmly in place.

I don't know your lover's mask. Does your mistress demand the same attentions as your wife? Do you tire of the furtive glances, looking over your shoulder, the dutiful foreplay to gain a release? Don't despair—isn't it the party's worship, the inspired glorification of goodness, that has become your new mistress now?

It's the last dance, a Viennese waltz, "Ein Wiener Walzer" plays on ... I move into your arms, a perfect stranger, and use my eyes to caress your masked face ... but is the will of a stranger enough against the might of the fascist party faithful?

The mask slips, the curtain falls ...

I stand my ground.

My dance with your devil is complete.

Shall I burn in hell?

# Mates

Two ducks—separate,
Swim side by side
In perfect unison.
Twin lights on the water
Synchronised until death,
An invisible silk thread,
Natural connection,
Distilled harmony,
Exquisite web of life.

# Mea Culpa

We sat at a crowded café.
At a table, (you know) the one that has one leg shorter than the others.
The coffee was too hot from an overzealous machine operator,
Instead, I drank in your eyes, the confusion, the starkness.
Your lips didn't move.
Yet I felt each word spoken,.
I sipped then savoured them,
And measured the taste of my crass debasement.

*The table protested my sad dysfunction.*
Your sensitive artisan hands sat in companionable silence.
I looked at my coffee hands stained from shrewish ill temper.
But rigid honesty and a trite apology were all I could offer.

I sipped my cooling coffee,
And the dregs ebbed inside me.
*The table was still broken.*
My cup drained, empty.

I walked away, taking my coffee hands and irritable pride.
*You stayed at the rickety table*, still,
With your intuitive, artistic hands
And my coffee-soaked mea culpa.

# Mockery Unplugged

"Do not mock me," said the fly to the spider.
"You may weave your splendid silken web,
But I can make mournful music with my wings.
I have many lenses to see my world clearly with,
And I can soar to places you may only dream about.
Nature has a way of redressing the balance."

## Mother and Child

Child, you suckled at the breast of my maternal outpourings
To see you grow strong and proud.
You drunk freely of my milk to sustain and
Nourish the good spirit that dwells inside you.
We looked into each other's eyes and recognised
That part of you that grew in me
That part of me that grew in you
And when you first smiled, the light of your joy
Radiated out, capturing your beauty of innocence.
I took your tiny hand in mine and felt the strength of our bond,
That special timeless love that is reborn and renewed,
That is simply shared between mother and child.

# No-World

Somewhere in another world, your life began as 14861.
You awoke from the warm womb that breathed life into you,
Your tiny hands reached out, your little mouth puckered,
The blue blindness of new eyes sought to nuzzle
At the breast of maternal outpourings,
A droplet of innocence eased its way down your silken cheek,
Formed at the rose of your lips. Birth mother, numbered 1486,
Gently stroked the tear away, before the instructors observed,
Wrote down your non-human reaction.

You flourished, strong as per design, did as others did, slept and played,
Contained in the growing room, its white controlled light,
Subliminal messages piped smoothly into your toddler awareness,
You, like countless others before, serene, composed.
The seed you were, potted, watered, fertilised
With the knowledge of a millennium of muses.

By the age of three, observations were frequently recorded.
Numbers dominated, controlled thought patterns.
Sleep became your hidden adventure, the dreams of the dream-time.
Shapes and colours danced up from your subconscious,
A kaleidoscope of images surged through,
In sleep, you created a feeling, an emotion; you smiled.

As time moved on, the measurers noted
Your heart was abnormally large.
Such imperfection, in a human, not tolerated.
The balance of being unequal.
The old Seer looked into your eyes.
They travelled beyond the dome to the No-World
Your strangeness was evident to her,
Mathematics could not explain it; it was not pure.
Therefore, it could not exist at all.
In you, she calmly recognised the ghosts of the primitives.

It was decided that a transplant to an artificial heart
Would restore your humanism to order.
It was effected straight away,
The new heartbeat strongly inside you,
But the swirl of dreams continued.
Numbers had come to mean nothing.
Your eyes, your hands, your legs, searched beyond,
Then the High Humans clinically decreed
Your non- human state.
The hatch would be opened to you.

You walked out to your doom.
It was the No-World.
The newness assailed you.
You stripped off your suit,
Driven to be at one with the earth.
You lay down, stretched out,
Embodied the grains of substance that washed you,

A baptism of colour startled you,
You lay still and felt the glow of the spirits that had called,
Touched by their warmth on your skin, answering a primeval desire.
You yelled, and in that yell contained
All the emotion and feeling that had long been denied.
Then you laughed out loud to the echo of the new world.
A rush of blood raced through your veins.
They may have replaced your heart,
But they could never replace your soul.

# O Jealousy

On the surface, I am becalmed.
The planes of my face carry smooth serenity.
There are no vestibules to carry waves of expression.
The winds of emotion have ceased into stillness.
A lull of quiet composure is preserved;
Indeed, my face has become a figurehead
Carved in classic wooden splendour.
I will not utter a sound.

But ask me what I feel inside.
Is it a willing meekness to inherit the earth?

No, my body churns with rage,
Storms of discomposure course through my veins.
Agitation awakens primal urges to take the offensive.
My body has become a *drakkar* ready for the initial attack.
I will charge against my imagined rival,
Carried by the dispossession of my vulnerable soul.
I will worship at the green altar of the Celtic monster
That lurks suspiciously within the troubled waters of my mind.

But this is wrong; I need to stay on an even keel.
I need a symbol of strength to ride the stormy currents.

Perhaps I'll look to the ancients to guide me?
I know—I will seek the design of unity and trinity

To bring forth the triple goddess
Of maid, mother, and crone.
The three planes of existence,
Physical, mental, spiritual interlocked,
An unbroken, joined circle of eternity
That embraced all land, sky, and sea.

Shall I get the triquetra tattooed on my arm to remind me?
Oh no—I'll carry it in my heart, mind, and soul instead.

# Ode to the Hugo Boss Man

I will dance this tango,
Solitary, alone as it should be,
Did you not understand the psychology?
The way of things? I guess not.
What? Did you expect me to dance to your tune ...?
This ballroom was never big enough for the both of us.

I will move to the rhythm of my own heartbeat,
Feel my stilettoed heels pound the wooden floor,
Glide to the side, step forward, then step back,
Swirl, sway, dip and turn,
Caught up in a sensuous stasis of dishevel,
All power to the de rigueur of freedom.

I will bend to the drumbeat, a seductive onslaught,
Feel the burnished glow of perspiration build,
Move to the heat, reach a climatic point,
Flick my hair in a careless wave,
Summon the call of independence,
It is as it should be—a wild, ruthless state.

I am not a bird to be caged,
And if I feel the steel bars enclose me,
It is because I allow it to be ...
I will not be trapped by words and gestures alone,
I need the music, the pulse of time;
Just leave me to my solitary state.

# Old Man

Old man lying in your hospital bed,
Cocooned in white cotton sheets,
So absorbed in your battle to survive;
The centre of your own universe.

Too afraid to live,
Fearful of death,
Just marking time ...

You hold no memories of a family torn asunder.
As an abuser of their bodies and minds
Left scars of self-doubt on their psyche,
Leeching off your children's life force.

Architecture was your occupation,
Womanising your preoccupation,
Whiskey your lifelong friend.

Until the final conclusion.
What do I feel for this father of mine?
Sadly, a dutiful pity,
With only a remote concern.

# One Tear

Composition: water, mineral salts, antibodies, and lysozymes

Water: gracious elixir of life, and we flowed, didn't we?
Just like Tom and Huck aboard that ramshackle raft,
Floating only on a hastily bound clump of small wooden sticks.
An aid in the lust for adventure, vivid dreams, ambitions,
Mischievous, gleeful discoveries, fishing; reeling them in.
Painting the whitewashed picket fences with deflected brightness,
Rainbows of colours swept on only by the limits of imagination.

Mineral salts: simple, inanimate, essential to keeping the balance of scales.
I bathed naked in your sea of antiquity under moonlight and felt the illumination
That only a semi-planet can give, as a token testament to its existence.
Rays of light, heat, mixing with the salts; omnipresent, keeping me lit and buoyant
So I floated on the crest of this impassioned wave, sustained by your salts of the earth. Dead Sea; you possessed me, abrasive, roughened hues of karma, under your control,
But, my dear, a little-known fact: salt combined with heat turns to ash when burned.

Antibodies: chained together in the proteomic fight to provide immunity in life.
So, what was I, the imperialistic invader who dared to breach the protection racket?

Set up by your body of works, a collection of tragedies, owing allegiance only to
The disquiet, unease, miscommunications created solely by projections and perceptions; a convenience of mind to deflect the true state of mind, I wonder?
Was I the itch that couldn't be scratched, the stubborn thorn expelled from the rose
That burrow unceremoniously under your skin, a continual irritation, pestering,
Festering the ferment of frustration that causes your body to defend, in effect?

Lysozymes: complex, cellular catalysts in the conditional constraints of reaction.
I'm one step removed, the fascinated voyeur, watching as you marshal your armies of enzymes, summon forth the antigens ready to neutralise, then feast upon the nucleus of my intent. I heard tell of the existence of good bacteria, but maybe in all your readings on science, ancient tales of fighting men, philosophy, and the search for the holiest of grails, you might have overlooked a 101 course in microbiology. Good bacteria does exist, asking nothing in return except to boost the fighting spirit that dwells inside your complex physiology, neurology, psychology and any other "ology" that takes your fancy.
In the end, it's just words, words that end in eulogy, with a full stop at the end.

This is one tear, the last tear I give to you; it is, what it is ... a tear for a dear friend.

# Open Arms

You opened your arms for me.
When I stopped, I paused then packed.
I left for your shores,
Blinded by delusion, then disgust
For the small-mindedness
That attacks the staunch,
The disenfranchised.

I stood and waved goodbye
To the chill of ill winds
That chased down yesterday's news
Through desolate streets,
Litter left over
As a testament
To society's contempt.

Yet I felt a smile
When I landed
On your shores.
Your arms engulfed me,
I felt secure
To reach up and out again
To the sky,
And bask in the spirit
Of your joy, O wondrous land.

# Plastic Fantastic

No longer comfortable with her image,
Ready to shed her skin.
Under the surgeon's knife,
Obsessed with the outside,
Spiritually bankrupt within.

Surface glitz and glamour
Skims her image of perfection,
A fading inner light.
She turns sideways
And almost disappears.

Never gives a full-faced smile
Lest a groove outlive its welcome.
Feels the poisonous injection
Freeze-frame her face.
Another generous donation
To her smiling plastic surgeon.

# Pretensions of Poetry

Focus on the banal, the inane,
The rudimentary.
Ignore the exposition, the exploration,
Of social commentary.

Put a mirror to modern verse.
Reflections of insular, depressive
Imagery.
Explore inwards with the
Greatest intensity
The human spirit, brimful
Of insecurity.

The "Old Masters" knew
How to focus on the true
Issues of consequence for their time.
The modern writer
Kneels before the altar
To worship Narcissus,
The forefather
Of modern rhyme.

## Protest song against dictatorship

Where are the songs,
The persistent drumbeat,
That rains down on his parade?
The lost age of Aquarius,
The verses of sublime protest,
Arms crossed, united and joined,
Stood tall, tough and strong
Against this insidious authoritarian rule.

Listen; the dictator marshals his henchmen.
The people stand meek in contemplation.
Then an eerie silence echoes through the land.
Off they march to the capital,
Using all possible false pretence.
Hide and disguise their true desires
Against the men, women, and children of democracy.
See the propaganda machine saturate their lands,
Touch the psychosis of the warped within the little orange man.
Feel the fires of hate rage on.

It's our inaction that carries
The burden of guilt,
Laid waste at our very own doorsteps.
We read about the horrors,
Digest our breakfast with the pictures,
Hear the radio blare with lost lives.
Yet still we continue on with our daily plan.
Oblivious to and desensitised from
The fate of democracy.
Please, please let there be a day when the people rise,
Against this dictatorship, the scourge of this beloved free land.

# Rain Chant

Please rain.
Give up your secrets.
Perhaps now?
My lips are sealed;
I do promise
I won't tell.
Yours is no simple whisper,
But a persistent drumbeat.
You pound loud, soft then loud.
My body feels the potency
Of your voodoo chant.
Why do you lure me so?
Your mystic forces form
A transcendency to enthral me
Your rhythmic symphony
Lulls me into illusion, then dance.
Capture me slowly and carefully
Under your witchdoctor's spell
Then let me fall then descend
Into nature's oratory trance.
Please rain.
I promise
To not tell.

# Reclusive Silence

Is it your howl I hear, my earth son?
That slides down inclines and slippery slopes,
Sweeping through the stands of forest pines,
Across the prickly plains of cacti and prairie grasses,
Riding the winding labyrinth of rivers and streams.

Do you test your distance from that most cursed of species: human beings?
Your radiated plea diminishes as time serves to dilute its intensity,
But it is your one note, nestled in the rest, the pauses, that offers crystalline
Clarity, where only true glory of solitude is borne and witnessed by me,
The mother of this earth and humble daughter to the vast divine universe.

Do you heed the hushed call? Feel the lure of the feral side, my boy,
Stalked the shadows of the wordless creatures that lurk tacitly
Under the rich herbaceous carpet, that mysterious mute covering
A blanket of green laid out in random systematic design
Nestled amongst the serene forests of noiseless antiquity.

Seek and you will find, my child.
As I let my nurturing trees wrap their green sleeves
Of fostering barked branches with delicate needlepoint leaves
To stroke and soothe your silent pain
That has stymied and enveloped your sense of worth.

Do partake of my generous bounty, little one,
Bath in the languid, tranquil streams,
Wash in the replenishment of life-affirming juices,
Float and let the benevolent sun's rays quietly caress you
And pillow your insecurities against man-made mentalities.

You swim against the current of life's stream, my sad one.
Break the flat surface skin and sink down into its depths,
Rest in the vacuous chamber that will insulate you
And hear nothing but the stoic rhythm of your organs
As they pay homage to your essential world within.

But when this has been done, my wild child,
And you have taken your quiet contemplation,
Heard the solicitous evening call of the coyote,
Seen the elk graze with serene grace and beauty,
I plead with you to bridge that essential gap
And make the trek back to humanity. They will need you.

# Refinement

And if I should one day see you
Leaned up against a wall
With one leg tucked behind the other
Positioned just so,
Half in light,
Half in shadow,
Displaying that elegant profile,
I'd walk right up to you,
Tilt my head slightly to the left,
Give the most quizzical look,
Place a quick peck on your cheek,
Smile ever so sweetly,
Then just saunter away.

# Rosebud

Intricate, delicate, divine,
Closely held secrets
Tucked tightly in bud.
What will it take to unfurl,
Feast up your essence,
Open upon your flagrant fragility,
Perfect bud of the rose?

Beauty in purpose,
Untouchable porcelain,
Yearning for that first exquisite touch.
The soft sigh of dew on your open silk petals
So delicate, exquisite, exposed.
Disarm me, assail me, and seduce me.
I quiver with the sensuous assault of expectation
To taste the touch of your beauty exposed.

# Self-Doubt and Communication

I'm working away in the still of the night,
The house echoes with a boomerang of thought.
Patterns of burden, responsibilities, doubt;
I carry the weight heavy on my mind.
The task I'm set is for a good cause, I think.
Please give me the strength to do it right.

Interruptions inevitably stem
The current of my concentration
With thoughts of you and I think,
Wouldn't it be nice just to hear your voice?
Yet I find I grow weary
Of that essential device—the modern telephone.
I work with them day and night,
I know their connections, their physiology,
Their essential organs constrained in a chassis,
The processors, compressors, and daughterboards,
And their applications that stalk the unworldly.

O Telecommunications with mass market appeal,
The tireless purveyor of interruptions,
The continuous flow of illusory interaction,
The exchange of numbers, transmission,
Talk, text, and artificial speech ...
They all gang up under the ruse of real conversation.
So I sigh and go back
To reviewing the data collected,
Plugging in the essential information,
Make allowances for the fixated configuration,
Think limitations, capacity, solution, delivery,
And wait for my thoughts to inevitably
Meander back to you; your written words
And our quaint lines of communication.

# Shh—The world need not know

Shh—The world turns ...
Bound, gagged, and hooded,
Trembling in the darkness of an unknown journey.
Hood removed, disintegrated by bloodied splattered walls.
Their calling card is a testimonial of intent,
And I smell the excrement of fear,
I hear the distant groans, a cat-chorus of despair.
You ask questions of me
That I have no answers to
You force my head down into the water.
I struggle, I splutter as I try to choke in empty air.
Is this the way I'll die?

Shh—The world still turns ...
You ask more questions I have no answers to.
You ask me over and over and over again,
You starve my body,
You starve my mind from inner light.
I peer through the darkness.
There aren't even four walls; I am deprived of all.
Is this the way I'll die?

Shh—The world is turning ...
You ask the same question over again.
I have no answers to tell.
I am dislocated, viewing from above.

My body is whipped into action
As flesh leaves my bones.
I hear the simple snap
Of the cracking of my joints
As you attempt to dismember my spirit.
Is this the way I'll die?

Shh—The world turns and turns ...
You ask no more questions
I never had answers to.
I lie here unmoved as I count down the minutes
For these torturous men to pay me a final visit
To end my dimming spirit once and for all.
This is the way I die.
Shh—Didn't you know? The world need not know ...

# Simple Love Poem

Let me write a simple poem,
Pure in its simplicity,
With words that speak honestly,
That provides a true intent.
Let me find some simple words
That explain quite openly
The simple words
That were once so easy
Scribbled on the page
So they may be
Spoken directly
To the one I love.

# States of Matter

The molten magma flows with intent and rises in expectation.
Burst, and flow, lava, flow down the slippery slopes of mountains
Or molehills, representing the double standards of creation.
Hot fluid in a loose lava state of matter
Or a rock-solid compound, bound to the earth's crust.

Yet you to seem apply these standards to me,
But with my spirit within, I have the flight of freedom.
I am grounded only by the need to feed my responsibilities,
Not bound by the principles of state and proprietary.
What you have doubled,
I have halved in response.

And I do whiff the gaseous cloud of suspicion
That surrounds the reflections of your form.
Racy liquid energy; or rock-solid dignity?
Does it really matter, ultimately?
As fate and faith overcome most perceptions.

I only ask that I may rest a time, on you, rock
As a bird weary from flight
Or observe from a distance
Your flow of molten energised creativity,
But do not apply the dualism that besets thee;
I am simple, really, my own standard, with a desire to ultimately fly free.

# Table Talk

We sat at a table
Sharing a last coffee
Before your take-off,
Your flight of fancy.
"Fancy that," you said
In beautiful even tones.
You even sipped your coffee,
So sartorial, refined.
While all the time,
My anger rising,
You gave your cool cat smile
Set in your mahogany veneer face
That matched the smoothness
Of that suit.
I longed for casual; T-shirt and jeans,
Just to smash the coating,
Hear a chuckle,
See it reach your eyes.
Clasp your hand,
Feel a pulse underneath.
You, sir,
This two-dimensional figure
Sitting elegantly cross-legged outside a coffee shop
And me just sat
Dragging on a ciggie
With cooling coffee
And musing about
Stubborn pride.

# Terminals—Flights

Another terminal, another departure.
The hollow clink of high heels on the worn walkway
Past omnipresent billboards, kiosks, shops.
Through the glass-encased community
In this damned insulated nameless town
With the continuous drone of industry's surround-sound
Broken by the muffled roar of jets overhead.

Bowed down by too many cities of late,
We are the walking wearied
Who muse with tired wonder
If there'll ever be connecting flights?
Perhaps a chance stopover or midnight sojourn
For two people who dream of one day
Robbing the redeye, that mind-numbing bird of prey.

We are, after all, the experimental mice
Bound by the treadmill of life.
The distance apart is marked, scheduled, maintained,
So these are the only constants that remain:
Separation, terminals, flights.
Icarus had the right idea;
Wings burnt by the sun's molten blight.

Because dreams simply dissolve with flight.

# Dedication to the Aspen Tree

The aspen tree reaches high.
It doesn't have to;
The sun bends to delicately touch its leaves,
Soft crystals of rain rest in respite on the canopy of coverings,
Severe winds call to the tree to gracefully bend and twist to its whistler's strains,
Wintery ice sheets cloak the wooden skeleton with time suspended still.
But it is the autumnal days that herald the spectacular carnival tints of red and yellow haze,
Ochre, cadmium, vermillion and alizarin crimson,
Boldest of beauty before the stillness of winter's rest.
It is said you cannot ever shade an aspen tree;
It is created to shine,
To paint on nature's magnificent canvas.

# The Clown

Roll up, roll up—see the amazing Bim Bom perform ...

Clown, when you clown around,
Do you silently laugh back at the audience when they laugh at you?
Of course you do.
Behind the painted-on smile and the thick made-up pancake face
Do they suspect your critical disdain with two sad teardrops drawn on?
Don't they know they're just a foil
For your two-act, one-man slapstick?
Do you think they ever suspect your razor-sharp mind
That lurks under the layers of silly circus costume and childish pomp?
Your actions speak louder than words.
A mute, consummate showman
Your performance to the world.
Yet you are the maestro, and you play them so.
Don't they know behind the smiles
You act on the violation of taboos,
You mock the sacred and profane,
Exploit the imaginations of their inner child?
And the ringmaster thinks he's in control,
The audience believes what they want to believe.
Well, the jokes on them, isn't it, Bim Bom the Clown?

# The Disappeared

**1**

I am your daughter, Mama.

Tell me you still see me,
That you carry a secret vision,
Even though I've disappeared.

Can you still hear me?
My excited chatter about my first date.

Do you still smell the delicate perfume
Of frangipani I wore in my hair?

Do you recall my last dance round the room?
Ready for that first real kiss
In my red grown up dress.

**2**

I am a bird, Mama.

I soar beyond the chambers of
Subjugation, torture, agony
These monstrous men inflict on me.

Let them beat me, kick me,
Tear me inside out.

Let them dispose of my ruined body.
They can no longer reach to touch me.
The shackles broke free.

The sky has called me ...

# The Family

The alley is long and straight.
There are no pauses, no deviations
To reveal the tunnelled mutation of our relations.
I crawl through the septic cesspit of waste,
Thick ghastly sewage that seeps out from your distortion of love.
Pitch black, hooded, disoriented, gasping for breath
As a toddler, given a tightrope, clumsily moving across your drawn line.

You're the full stop at the end, or so you think.
Vivid eyes fixated, mesmerised, drawn with no flame
To the swelling outline, the shadowed bloom of custodial rights,
The bulging shrinkage of your hopes, dreams, fascinations
Recycling the Family's dissipation of yet another generation.
I have accommodated the incubation of your distorted paternalistic ideal;
Madonna and unborn child, violent immaculate conception
To become the flawed, fated possession, carrying a possession's child.

The end is nigh; press on, O mournful hymn of inevitability.
The Athenian Cassandra knew, didn't she, the prospect of doom.
Pray stop; myths have no reality in the fight for the spirit's life.
Do not cower; stand upright, for the innocent hope that grows inside you,
A featherlike connection of a fragile fetus foot,
The boxer's kick that imprints so strongly against your embattled heart.
Walk now strongly where destinations are measured in the courage of feet,
March to the beat of defiance and turn a perception of defeat into power,
Utilise the element of surprise, tip the chess board over and simply
turn away.

# The Forgotten

I am a child of war; tell me what that means?
Don't quite understand about friend or enemy.
Do you love some people and hate others?
I'm only eight years of age.

Anah is my best friend; he's a Sunni.
But Father says he's now the enemy.
The Yankee soldiers shoot like the enemy.
But Father says they're now our friends.

I'm lucky; we have guns for real.
We don't need sissy computer games.
My father and brother are in the people's army.
Yay! They shoot for real each day.

My oldest brother went to heaven last week.
Didn't understand why they cried and cried.
Shouldn't they have all laughed and smiled
Because he went to Allah's place to live?

Mother doesn't give me smiles or hugs anymore.
She just sits all day with a funny look on her face,
Calling my brother's name over and over again,
With big wet tears in her eyes.

My other brother drinks and sniffs funny stuff,
His eyes go all yucky and crazy.
He says he wants to blow up the world,
But I worry because I'm in it.

I am a child of war,
Now I think I know what it means.
It's about grown-ups and their things,
And how we children get in the way!

# Impressionists

You have a silent acceptance of me,
You do not ask questions, expect answers I'm not prepared to give.
I understand this as an unequal affair;
There have been many who have fallen for your promise of romance.

How is it that my childish delight can regenerate each year at the thought of seeing you?
The giddy expectation we will meet on yet another first date,
With my smile, my gypsy enthusiasm, I capture your attention; send a passionate kiss to your culture,
drink in your maturity, and delicately run my fingertips over your embrace.

I simply view you as a plein-air painting, rendering your light.
You make me feel nearly beautiful in return.
I breathe in your panoramic vision,
I dare not see your: faults, scars, small transgressions,
Is it so wrong to capture on the canvas of my mind,
The impressions, the beauty as a whole?

I do not view as trite the ocular dysfunction
of such artists of perfection as: Monet, Renoir, and Cézanne.
To disregard perspective offers: liberation of feeling, a grace of being,
a suspension of time.

# The Joker

The painting stood centrestage,
A vision of colour.
Pure lines,
Simplistic, almost childlike in form.
Showing a mastery of technique,
Critics said.
An unknown artist
Starving for recognition?
No, actually my four-year-old son
Tucked up in bed.

# The Liverpool Kid

He stood on the street corner, a typical Sunday afternoon,
In tattered singlet, shorts, and jandals, with a bottle of coke,
a pack of cigarettes,
And his fighting words—punch-drunk from a succession of fights
going on in his head.

Perched on my ringside seat with horrified fascination,
Insulated by the glass frontage of the Subway Café, I watched his
contorted mouth move—yet strangely silent, trying to pick up the
abuse hurled at any passerby.

The "Liverpool Kid", by name and reputation,
Got his willing mark by provocation and reliving his glory days,
Managed to pulverise his opponent—
by smashing his head against the ground.

The Kid raised his arms in victory to the stunned crowd that had gathered
around, not a scratch to be seen, just a torn singlet and a broken jandal,
Such a pity—about the mangled brain inside his head.

# Ode to the Working Mum

The shrill blast of the alarm clock,
Her head stuffed under a pillow,
Shutting out the new day.
Five minutes of borrowed time
After a night of interrupted sleep,
A restless baby with a tooth finally through.

She rises, shaking off the lethargy,
Switching on to autopilot mode.
Showered and dressed, no time to spare,
She stares at her reflection:
A drab canvas until make-up is applied.

An early starter of coffee and vitamins,
The children quickly given breakfast and dressed.
A whirl of activity, debris swept away,
Children deposited at the school bus,
Baby dropped off at crèche.

A fight to get on the freeway,
The car her weapon
In this daily battle to get to work.
Traffic jams, the incessant blasting of horns,
Etching ever closer
Her heartbeat races
Got to beat the clock
Her mantra is reaffirmed.

Another shot of coffee,
Reports to be completed.
The soft drone of industry's surround-sound
An inevitable round of meetings,
Her polite façade fixed in place.
Overlooked for promotion,
Multi-tasking not appreciated
As much as male testosterone.

A quick glance of her watch;
The end of an "official" working day.
Her mask begins to slip, make-up slightly smudged
With the inevitable fight on the freeway
As kids bundled into the car
For the return trip home.

A hive of activity,
Chaos brought to some order,
Baby washed and fed,
Children sat in front of the TV,
Husband arrives home later,
Empty gestures of assistance,
Family sits down for tea.

Finally, quietness descends,
Children tucked up in bed,
They stare at each other.
Individual thoughts focused on the day,
All desire washed away,
In an ocean of fatigue,
Time to prepare for bed,
For yet another working day.

# The man who carried round his neatly wrapped box

**1**

John Steinbeck travelled east to his guilt-stricken Eden.
Did Dostoevsky's crime fit the punishment, I wonder?
Oh Edgar, was the eye really to blame?
Walk to your death ...
Wash the blood off your hands, Lady Macbeth!

**2**

So, let's assemble the accused and the accuser.
Let opposing side choose a punishment.
Let the will of the people decide.
To wit, they decided there was no case to answer
(Even though he carried round a strange little box)!
In the Socratic way, he was mercifully set free.

# The Pond

Stone thrown
Into a glass pond.
Ripples and reverberations
Radiate out in seismic motion.
Circular cataclysmic waves
Breaking over consciousness and consequences
Culminating in the chaos of creation.

# The Tree

The tree stands tall and proud.
It hears the echoes of children past, giggling,
Their peals of laughter
As they clamber up and over
Or hang down from its boughs.

Its generous swathe of green
Has served a generation of babies
Laid innocently out on a blanket
Under the tree's protective leafy canopy,
Touched by the warmth of filtered autumn sun.

It has heard the sobs of a jilted lover
Who has grazed her fingers lightly over
The tattoo of a heart and initials
That has been etched so deeply, so permanently,
At the foot of the fine old tree.

Many times, it has provided the solace, the sanctuary,
The stillness, the silence,
For the family member who has leaned back
Against its solidness, to garner enjoyment
From thoughtfully sitting, or simply reading a book.

It has heard the deepest anguish,
The howls of a devoted mother, torn apart,
Clutching the letter
That states, regrettably, her son
Will no longer be returning from war.

The old man, wheelchair-bound,
Sits under the grand tree.
He gazes over to the family home,
He sucks back on his pipe,
He gives a soft smile as he blows out the smoke.
Very slowly he closes his eyes,
He sees what the tree sees.
The tree stands tall and proud.

# The Moth, the Moon, and the False Light

The moth flies round the light.
Fly, moth, fly, until you see the folly.
You're caught with no reason why?
Nature's curse is that it deems it so.
Navigation, perhaps, to good purpose,
The source of an inspired compass,
Just as the moon's glow may guide you.

But beware the circle of reflected light
With no purity, just false lured intent.
Is it the trap, a voyeur's peek at your flight?
Are you just a mere object of cynical regard?
An amusing interlude to view your pathetic attempts,
Your futile dance of winged despair captured within
The endless cycles of grief that enslaves you.

And I see the moth, the moon, and the false light
As an illumination on my computer screen.
"The 0s and 1s in their infinite arrangements."
But there is no "sweet voice" to be perfectly parroted,
Just an endless shrill of sad senseless squawks
As you de-hand the hand of friendship
Because courage and goodness deserted you
As the shadow returns, but do not despair, my dear,
Suspicion and accusation will continue to light you.

# Immersion

The forest rests in the half-light.
Trees neither awake nor asleep,
A spirit dreamtime where
Haunting appearance summons serenity.
Mist shrouds their ghostly dance
As they glide and swirl
To the forest concerto.
Secret sounds of beautiful silence,
Refracted waves of light,
Before the immersion of white
That draws in, wisdom of Mother Earth
A merging of the spirits with the land.

# There Was a Boy

There was a boy.
He was born beautiful.
His mother beamed with pride.
His father wondered why?
His son was destined to become one …
Forced to wear their prejudices, perceptions
As a barcode, subtle and subliminal, on his forehead.

In his youth, he shrugged it off nonchalantly.
"Let them see me as they want to see me."
"Small images of lines, with spatial expectations,"
"I am me; I am free, they cannot reach me."
He soon learnt about the illusion of freedom.

As he grew older, the attraction grew.
The barcode became fully edged and inscribed.
"Let them read me as they want to read me."
"Read my lines, interrupt my plot summaries."
"I am me; I will read sonnets, read people."
He decided he liked reading sonnets more.

Now he is in middle age and irresistible.
The barcode is alluring and fully magnetised.
"Let them hear me as they want to hear me."
"Hear my pauses, the scripted melodies, those music thieves."
"They crowd me, surround me, consume me, engulf me."
"I am me; they don't see me, know me or hear me."
"I have become an imposed identity, exiled from the ordinary."

# Retro

Those were the days of the old school dances,
When the disco ball hung resplendent in the centre of the hall,
Where the girls had long hair, skimpy skirts with never-ending legs.
Bunched together, sizing up the boys, taking furtive glances.
As the boys strutted around like they were all that,
With their slicked-back hair, crazy flares. and buttoned-down paisley shirts.
And as the groove got up, the psychedelic lights kicked in,
Arms and legs moving in all directions, trying to keep with the vibe,
While continuing to check out who they fancied.
Supping down the cool sustenance of the spiked punch.
Letting inhibitions go and dancing with the moment.
Where did they go—I think it's now called retro.

## Thursday: 8.00 pm

You are not here.
Perhaps you are?
It is calm tonight.
I stand on the balcony;
A stranger's apartment
In a city that sleeps by night.
Civil servants at home tucked up
Snug in their plastic glass houses.
I drag on a cigarette.
My air is frigid,
A stark reality
Eased by the glowing tip.
Still, this business is a chessboard;
Black or white, no shades of grey.
The boys in bloated suits know it.
I am the pawn,
They are the pieces.
I got to watch them all day
Move over and around each other.
They miss the value of a pawn
To move at will.
They will find out tomorrow,
But it was you.
What were you?
That rendered me
Still,

Exposed,
Captured by en passant.
Hell
I fell
You looked back,
Returned,
I did battle with you on another level.
O sweet conflict,
You taught me to stand again
Then went
There are no clichés
Just memories.
Your infectious laugh,
Your soft touch,
Your essence of you.
The cigarette compensates.
The wheels of commerce will churn tomorrow.
Still,
I miss you.

# Transparent Moments

It's the eye of the storm,
When calmness prevails.
A temporary time-out
Until chaos returns
The dynamics of life.
A "transparent moment"
When balance is reached,
A short interlude of stasis
Until life intrudes.

A smile bubbles forth,
Worries placed on hold.
For this one special moment,
Peace infiltrates the soul.

# Unrequited Lust

A nameless person,
A chance encounter,
A sparkling winter's day.
An anonymous Paris street,
A perfect stranger,
A beautiful face.

Eyes drawn to each other.
Transfixed in a wisp of time.
His enquiring look?
A blush in response.
A shrug of my shoulders.
I move on.

# Vincent

Unlined face,
Not marred by reality.
Peter Pan,
Your own time warp.
Left your wife and kids at twenty-nine.
Never did return.

Artistic endeavour
To the extreme.
Brilliance, bordering on insanity,
Anaesthetic booze lines your soul,
Suspended in a world of your choosing.

Locked in;
A caricature of life.
Two-dimensional brushstrokes
Holding back your hand.
Never sullied,
In case the real-world returns.

# Birds of a Feather

We are birds of a feather. Mine from the spiritual sense. You because you actually do have feathers, a glorious plumage of vibrant orange and green. When I'm sitting at the keyboard, you find your way through the maze of my hair to place light little birdie kisses on my neck. Once you are bored with that, you use your head to nuzzle at the place where my neck and the ear join. I'm ticklish there and you respond to it. I know it as attention you seek or perhaps a reaffirmation that my love for you is constant.

I stroke you and then move you on to the keyboard. This is where you strut your stuff. You dance all over it on awkward legs, your claws attempting to balance on the rise and fall of the individual keys. You mumble indistinguishable sounds, interspersed with the odd word that sounds like a grumpy old man unhappy with proceedings. I laugh; you laugh too, just the way I do. We laugh at each other in that raucous way that friends do, without the pretence or self-consciousness that stilts honest communication. Your final destination is usually the top of my head. I feel you pluck away at my hair. I wonder if this is your instinctual memory of what a nest must have felt like.

Your time in a nest was always doomed. The moment the gum tree was split in two by an unseasonal and particularly ferocious southerly storm, you survived your fall, along with your sibling. But you were touched by human hands, and your mother, no doubt driven away by fear, deserted you.

You both came into my care that night, where there seemed to be an endless stream of hungry mouths to feed as kids and visitors combined to tell me about their day or to act as bearers of news.

The kindly park ranger walked into my mayhem clutching a cardboard box lined with ripped pieces of newspaper. Nestled in there, looking odd in an ugly bare and touchingly vulnerable way, your mouths remained gaped, issuing little squawks of desperation. At that moment, I was confronted with an age-old question: do I interfere with nature and rear you, with the inevitable result that your freedom would be denied? There was only a split second of doubt. Either by accident or design, the fates had conspired to send you to me; you had entered my house and you would not be turned away.

You both grew strong on a diet of cereal, pureed fruit, and baby food. Initially, your demands were constant, but as the weeks wore on, you both settled into a pattern of growth. Yet it was you, Dickhead, that sought extra comfort. You developed the strange habit of wanting to being carried around. Whether it was in the front of my sweatshirt, with your head just popping through from where it was zipped up, or just resting on my shoulder, you seemed to crave the motion. I began to seriously fear that you would become the first rainbow lorikeet in existence not to fly.

Your sibling, by contrast, displayed all the normal characteristics of a fledgling bird. It had happened smoothly and naturally. I craved normality for you, too, so I weaned you off the behaviour cycle that had seemed to slow your development. I took full responsibility for your retardation. To call you a slow learner was an understatement, but eventually, you got those wings into motion.

It was during this time that I buckled when I was asked by a friend if she could have one of you. She was a kindred spirit, and I knew whichever bird she got, it would be well looked after. The decision to keep you, Dickhead, was in reality no decision at all. It was hard to resist your cheekiness and the funny way you'd tilt your head as though you were listening intently to whatever I was saying.

By then, your answering squawks had turned into a rich variety of whistles and songs. You were allowed the freedom of the house, but you had to be caged when placed outside during the day, while I was at work. I had purchased the biggest cage I could find, but it still left me with a huge sense of guilt, seeing you through the thin steel bars. I also knew that as a hand-reared bird, you would have very little chance of surviving out in the wild.

But I learnt that, even with you, the drive for freedom becomes a powerful lure. Your first escape happened when your cage was being cleaned out and you managed to push your water container up and out from where it was held in place. It provided enough space for you to crawl through. I can only say it was planned with precision, and the next thing I knew, you were standing on the verandah looking up at me. We stared at each other, and I called your name gently, bending down, letting you see my shoulder, with the dwindling hope you would hop on to it. You didn't. You just flew up into the nearby trees and gave me a repertoire of your whistles. You remained there for several minutes before you launched yourself into the unknown.

Unfortunately, your timing was off. It rained heavily for each successive night. During the day I'd call out to you, and I'd hear a distant answering call. I'd try to discern from which direction it was coming. It gave me a small window of hope that you would make you way back to me.

It was early on the morning of the third day I was awoken by a series of grumbles, mumbles, squawks, and screeches from what sounded like a neighbour's tree. It was unrelenting, and you sounded bereaved and hungry. I don't think you allowed many people in the neighbourhood to sleep in that morning. I hurriedly got dressed and was greeted by the neighbour across the road trying to lure you down from their tree with the promise of an apple. You resisted but kept up a cavalcade of mournful squawks. It took an hour of talking to you and whetting your appetite with the fruit, but eventually, your stomach got the better of you and you flew on to my shoulder and I walked you home. You've left me several times since then. Each time, the same routine. Each time, your empty stomach outweighs nature's call. On one occasion, I just opened your cage door. I don't know what motivated me. Was it a morbid curiosity or was I simply racked with guilt?

However, something about that first time away changed you. Your behaviour became more bizarre. Like a child learning their first words where they always seem to regurgitate the swearwords first, you cultivated an impressive list. One day, while following me around in the kitchen, you picked up a new Chux cloth and carried it around with you. You haven't stopped since. Every week I give you a fresh cloth to play with. I sigh when I see you with it, dragging it around like some bird version of a security blanket. I even see you lying on your back, on the floor of the cage, tossing it around and around. You squawk endlessly if it is taken away from you. Do I want you to perch like a normal bird? Yes, I do. Do I want you to fly with your brethren? Yes, I do. Do I want you to act as a normal bird? Yes, I do. But somewhere along the way, there was a disconnect from the natural world, and you became a big part of my world.

I used to feel remorse that, in saving you, I may have turned you into something akin to a freak in a circus sideshow. Now, I guess you could say we've reached a plateau of understanding. It's as though the Chux cloth anchors you to me. There's something inside you that won't allow you to sacrifice the cloth in favour of your freedom. Your cage door is always open now. It is your retreat.

Your swearing has eased off, but your vocabulary has broadened. You know you own name, and you call me by mine. You say hello when the telephone rings and you even give a convincing imitation of Snoopy's bark. But it's your ability to give affection, the comical set of your head when I speak to you, your series of mumbles and grumbles as you search out new horizons in the house, and your unfailing willingness to stay with me even though the cage door is always open that fill me with wonder at your intelligence, but also a tinge of regret that in some way I have denied you your natural-born right to a bird's life.

# When a Man Despises a Woman and Vice Versa

A man.
A woman.
A 22-year-old son.
A perfect family,
A pretty portrait
Painted over too many times.

She's seeking
Emotional gratification.
A series of one-night stands.
Relief found in the bottom of a bottle.
Searching, searching ...
An endless buzz of excitement
Poised on an emotional tightrope.

He closes off
The world around him.
An island
Solely dedicated to his son.
Searching, searching ...
For the childhood
That should have been.

Assets and habits,
Divided lives,
Bitter adversaries.
Their son
Searching, searching ...
For release
From this perpetual mind-field.

# When one has lived a long time within the maddening crowd

When one has lived a long time within the maddening crowd
The sound of silence plays wondrous music to the ears
Builds to the pauses became one long
Onset of rapture
A note to dreaming
White noise oblivion, we just stand
When one has lived a long time within the maddening crowd.

When one has lived a long time within the maddening crowd
The wildflower on the sidewalk pokes its head up without fear
Of the human condition to destroy
It is born to grow
Because it knows
By its very nature it commands regard, we just treasure
When one has lived a long time within the maddening crowd.

When one has lived a long time within the maddening crowd
The stare of a stricken sparrow stunned
By the glass of human containment
Requires one to pause
Let the stare subside
To view the open door, we just understand
When one has lived a long time within the maddening crowd.

When one has lived a long time within the maddening crowd
Passion becomes constrained

By expectation, materialism, loyalties, and doubts
Strength becomes weakness, a foible
Egos conspire to create
Humility is lost within the milieu, we are just confused
When one has lived a long time within the maddening crowd.

When one has lived a long time within the maddening crowd
One decides that moments of joy are to be grasped with both hands
Constructed by simple things
Family, pets, loving friends
Silly moments
Beautiful winter days, a chorus of city songbirds, we just embrace
When one has lived a long time within the maddening crowd.

When one has lived a long time within the maddening crowd
Love becomes a strange thing
Overused, commercialised
Connections made and lost, then perhaps re-established
Purity of emotion becomes stagnant
With pride and suspiciousness, we forget about respect
When one has lived a long time within the maddening crowd.

When one has lived a long time within the maddening crowd
One realises it's not one but we
From bonny babies to boisterous great-grannies
We just are
We
Living a long time within the maddening crowd.

## Woman to Woman

Venus flytrap diviner
Open your leaves, cilia projections
Is it knowledge we seek
Above all else?
Transience of time?
Innocence of dawn?
Childlike wonder?

An ache of absence calls
Devoid of nervous system or tendons
So softly tighten your trap
Dissolve my inner parts
Leave my skeleton longer
For soft sultry secretions
To squeeze the aromatic juices
Empty my soul
Then close shut
The yearn, churn, burn.

# Worm performing the capoeira while I'm hanging out the washing

Oh, worm performing your dire Afro-Brazilian fighting dance,
    You are within the combat zone;
    I'm the accidental spectator that joins you;
    I hear the mystical strains of a litany,
    Nature's incantatory recital.
    Your cedar skin is burnished by the sun,
    The oppressive light has enslaved you;
    I see it too clearly now.

    Your dance of the desperate capoeira,
    Solo; fluid, acrobatic, ground play.
    You look so alluringly vulnerable;
    Brown boneless body rocking back and forth.
    What is it that ails you?
    That you can't find your way out of the *roda*,
    This all-consuming circle?
    Do you seek the shelter of blunt grass?

Stretch out your length
Until you have back the strength
To burrow downwards again.
Shall I intervene?
The conga drums are pounding slower now
Do I have the will to remain an enthralled observer?
Can I watch this lethal dancing game where death seems inevitable?
The songs reverberate now, waiting for a reply.
I cannot, in all conscience, respond.
I move slowly out of the *roda*.
She has won ...
And I walk away.

# Yesterday's News

She used to feel pain
Gut wrenching anguish
The hurt was never imagined
The anger was real
She even bled on the page
Now she feels nothing
"If only" doesn't exist
Read the **Headlines,** buster
You're yesterday's news.

# If Only

If only you could see
To see the light before your eyes.

If only you could feel
To feel the warmth of another.

If only you could touch
To touch the soul that calls you.

If only you could taste
To taste the salt of her skin.

But you never could, you never tried;
She called it existing, you called it living.

There's no going back.
The clock can't tock tick.

## Chess Pieces

Chessboard pieces
Black or white; no shades of grey
There are no fairy pieces in this game's set-up
Oh yes, we understand, or do we?
Pawns are moved at will
Never underestimate the value of a pawn's will
An en passant can offer many surprises
Eight pawns, not pieces
Eight ways to make endless plays
Forget the other pieces
It's become so easy to up-end the board
And simply walk away.

www.ingramcontent.com/pod-product-compliance
Lightning Source LLC
Chambersburg PA
CBHW050418120526
44590CB00015B/2014